THE PERSONAL TOUCH

Encouraging Others Through Hospitality

by Rachael Crabb
with Raeann Hart

Foreword by Larry Crabb

NAVPRESS

A MINISTRY OF THE NAVIGATORS
P.O.BOX 35001, COLORADO SPRINGS, CO 80935

The Navigators is an international Christian
organization. Jesus Christ gave His followers
the Great Commission to go and make
disciples (Matthew 28:19). The aim of The
Navigators is to help fulfill that commission by multiplying laborers for Christ in
every nation.

NavPress is the publishing ministry of The
Navigators. NavPress publications are tools
to help Christians grow. Although publications alone cannot make disciples or change
lives, they can help believers learn biblical
discipleship, and apply what they learn to
their lives and ministries.

Library of Congress Catalog Card Number:
     90-63217
ISBN 08910-96078

Third printing, 1993

Cover design: Kent Puckett Associates

Printed in the United States of America

CONTENTS

AUTHORS

Rachael Crabb grew up in York, Pennsylvania, and taught elementary school in Champaign, Illinois, after graduating from West Chester State College. She also taught at the preschool level in Boca Raton, Florida, and holds an M.A. degree in early childhood education.

Rachael has been involved in the Stonecroft Ministries as a regional representative in Florida and Indiana. She has served as the director of women's ministries at a church in Warsaw, Indiana, and as a member of the Parent's Cabinet at Taylor University. She speaks on a regular basis for women's retreats. Rachael and her husband, Larry, live in Denver, Colorado, and are the parents of two grown sons, Keplen and Kenton.

Raeann Hart is a writer and former editor of a Christian magazine. She has published numerous articles and poems in a variety of magazines. Raeann resides in Warsaw, Indiana, with her husband, Albert, and their four children—Kyle, Rick, Tiffany, and Remington. Raeann and Albert own and operate Hart & Hart Advertising Agency.

FOREWORD

To the best of my knowledge, no one has written a manual for a husband writing a foreword for his wife's book. I'm sure other men have done what I'm about to do, but they haven't passed along guidelines to those who would later follow in their path. So, with the advantages of neither coaching nor precedent to help me do it correctly, I'll just say what I really think about *The Personal Touch* and its author, my wife.

I wish people who read this book could experience the everyday reality of our home life. Sometimes (not very often) we're bored—bored with an evening, bored with ourselves, bored with life in general. Far more often, we'd prefer the opportunity to feel a little bored. Our lives are full with hectic schedules, people whom we want to see and who want to see us, plumbers who arrive three hours late, and several hours at a time in the dentist's chair.

Occasionally, we're overwhelmed with heavy responsibilities, with criticism that stings, with news that literally tears our hearts into pieces, or with tension with close friends that we have no idea how to handle.

There are, however, several constants in our lives. As I reflect on *The Personal Touch*, the one constant that stands out to me is this: My wife is always thinking of people. This is evident in her conversations:

> To me she says, "Wait! Before we go to their house, I want to get the gift I bought last week for their new baby."

> On the phone she asks, "When are you flying in? Look, I'll pick you up. I'm spending the day with a friend's daughter who is in town for several days. It'll be good for the three of us to spend a little time together."

> To the saleslady in our home she suggests, "Since you're having such a hard time finding a church, why don't I pick you up Sunday after next, and we'll go to church together."

Sometimes I'll suggest that we include friends in our evening dinner plans at a restaurant, and she'll sigh, then quietly say, "I'd rather be with just you. I feel like we haven't been alone in weeks."

Rachael is one of those few Christians who live in the center of their gift. If hospitality is properly defined not only in terms of entertaining in one's home but also (and far more importantly) as an other-centered engagement with people that comes as naturally as breathing, then that is her gift. Several times a month I'll stop and notice the dozens of ways Rachael expresses her love for people, then look at her and say, "You're remarkable."

Rachael has her flaws. (I don't need rose-colored glasses to appreciate her.) But she understands the value of encouragement, and she has learned a difficult lesson about encouragement: The best way to handle the hurt of not getting it is to give it.

Giving encouragement is more important than many of us often realize. What we call psychological problems are, in most cases, the product of painful, self-centered relationships. People have been hurt, and they spend most of their energy seeing to it that they don't get hurt again.

Nothing breaks into that cycle of "You've hurt me, now I'll back away from you" quite like loving encouragement. I'd like to see Christians learn to give themselves to others in the opportunities of everyday life rather than see ten new counseling centers established.

That's why I think this book is important. It addresses in doable, practical terms one of the most critical needs in our world today: the need for encouragement that draws people to the Source of love by providing a little taste of what is available. Little things—a remembered birthday, taking a friend's daughter to lunch, a well-timed smile, a comment that says you've paid attention to what someone else is feeling—have probably done as much to free people to pursue our Lord as good preaching and insightful counseling.

That shouldn't surprise us. After all, the center of Christianity is love expressed in relationships, beginning with God's love to us in Christ and flowing into our love for Him and others.

The Personal Touch brings the richest truth of life down to a level where each of us can meaningfully participate in it. The fact that it's written by the woman I love most in the world may not have much to do with the book's value. (Remember, no manual tells me what I'm supposed to say in this foreword to my wife's book.) But the fact that hundreds of lives have been touched by a woman who is living out the message of encouragement is, I think, one good reason among many to read this book and take it seriously.

—LARRY CRABB

ACKNOWLEDGMENTS

Writing this acknowledgment feels, in one way, like standing behind the podium after receiving a longed-for, but unexpected, Oscar. Whom do I thank? Will I forget anyone?

I want to thank *all* of the individuals who selflessly offered hospitality to me and my family and encouraged me greatly by showing the kind of encouraging love of which the Bible speaks. I can name only a few; the entire list would be a book in itself. Thanks to the folks at Stratford Park Bible Chapel in Champaign, Illinois, who took in newlyweds and, among other things, taught me to ask the butcher for rump roasts instead of picking out flat roasts from the meat case. Thanks, also, to the neighbors in Boca Raton, Florida, who had higher electric bills than we because they prepared so many meals for us. Right, Everetts and Caruanas?

I want to thank Toni Barnhill, who kept the birthday club going and hosted imaginative. parties, giving me great ideas for games and theme parties. Thanks to Wyn Porter, the gal of the ice breakers at the super seniors where my parents, Howard and Helen Lankford, have Friday lunch—I've used many ideas similar to Wyn's.

Of course, I want to thank Raeann and her family for the patience to work long distance, at times, on this book. I chuckle whenever I think of our first "secret" meeting to plan this project. We didn't tell a soul what we were doing, and in walked my husband and the interns from the counseling program. Larry casually but pointedly asked what Raeann and I were doing. I shared our hopes for this book with Larry a few months later when the secret get-togethers were conducted after Raeann's children were in bed—nine p.m. to midnight.

I want to thank Larry for being an encourager as I so often muddle through things. He has been a good friend for over thirty years, and I can honestly say that he has had the greatest positive impact on me. I'm fortunate to be his wife, and I *know* he's a strong, godly man who practices what he preaches. I am biased; I love and respect him! I also love two other men, Kep and Ken, our sons. They, along with their father, have made hospitality fun and, therefore, have been big contributors to this book.

Some names have been changed in this book, but the ideas and stories come from real people whom I appreciate and who have been a source of encouragement. Thanks to you. I trust you recognize yourselves.

Finally, I want to thank my editor, Traci Mullins, for enjoying my duets with Larry and for editing this book in such a way that the revisions were more fun to do than the first draft. Also, thanks to the terrific group at NavPress who make an outsider feel at home.

Chapter 1

❖

HOSPITALITY
WITH A PURPOSE

I was awakened in the middle of the night by a persistent knock at the front door. I groped my way down the hall and opened the door to find a police officer standing on my doorstep.

"Do you know this girl?" he asked.

Even if I'd had my glasses on, I'm not sure I could have recognized the thin teenager standing there. Her face was badly bruised and swollen, as if she had been in a car accident.

"I'm sorry; I don't think I do," I replied.

"Her boyfriend beat her up, and she says she has nowhere else to go," the policeman informed me. "You are the only people she knows who would give her a place to sleep. We don't want to put her in the county jail."

"Don't you remember me? I'm Kathy," the girl murmured weakly.

"Sure, I remember you. Come in."

My mind raced. What small act of kindness—a cup of hot chocolate, a cold drink, a meal in our home—had kept our memory alive in Kathy's mind? Years later when in a desperate situation, we were the only people she could think of who would take her in. I wondered what she would have done if we had never been friendly to her years before. I also shuddered to think of how many other Kathys there must be in the world.

Kathy stayed with us for a few days. I took her to the hospital for x-rays and medication. She went to church with us and apologized because she thought her clothes were not suitable. She finally went back to her boyfriend and stayed with him until he beat her again. Eventually, she found the courage to leave him and begin a new life.

Kathy still keeps in touch. She is married now and finally has begun to grow closer to the Lord. Last year she enclosed a check for five dollars to repay us for money we didn't remember giving her and had never missed. She said that experiencing our care for her made her think perhaps God could really care for her as well. This is an excerpt from her last letter to me:

> I'm not a Christian but I still believe in God and hope someday to be one of His children. I thank both of you very much for praying and having some of your thoughts on me. I needed so badly for God's help when I had problems. But I didn't always go to Him. But with the help of my Christian friends praying and thinking about me, He has helped. I really appreciate the time when you opened up your heart and home for me.

Hospitality is not always as dramatic as meeting a policeman at your front door and accepting a visitor in the middle of the night. Sometimes it is just making your home available for a Bible study, a church fellowship, or a party for your children and their friends. It can be having a quick cup of coffee with a coworker over a restaurant counter or serving an elegant dinner for dear friends. Whether in a phone call, in a note, or during an impromptu conversation, hospitality can be as simple as a kind word or taking some time to really listen to another person. Whatever the means, the goal should be the same: to *encourage* others.

A MINISTRY OF ENCOURAGEMENT

I met Elizabeth when I picked her up to come to our house for a visit. She had thick black hair and a porcelain complexion, with a few freckles scattered across her nose. When I first looked into her big blue eyes, I saw secrets and pain. Her guarded look made me think she had seen and experienced much more than she should have in her sixteen years of life. She watched me fix supper that evening and played with my young sons, Keplen and Kenton. Elizabeth was to spend a great deal of the next two years with our family.

I must admit I got to know Elizabeth at first out of desperation. Her mother, Catherine, was a disruptive member of our Bible study group. With ten children, she always had a serious problem that seemed to keep our Bible study group from learning about anything other than Catherine's personal problems.

After a few frustrating weeks, I finally called the leader of the group and we met together to pray. "Lord, please help me," I prayed. "Please send Your love for Catherine through me."

I am not a physically demonstrative person, so you can imagine my surprise at how the Lord answered my prayer. At our next Bible study, I found myself putting my arm around someone as I was visiting with the other women. As my eyes traveled down my arm, I realized it was around Catherine! I was actually beginning to have real Christian love and compassion for this woman.

As I began to listen, I realized that her daughter Elizabeth was a major concern to her. I was taking one of my husband Larry's counseling classes at the time. We were each assigned a "community client," so I decided to "adopt" Elizabeth. After our first visit, Elizabeth became a regular guest at our home.

I usually invited a dozen people to have dinner with us each Wednesday evening before we attended Larry's counseling class. Elizabeth became my regular assistant in the kitchen, and she watched my sons while I attended class. Eventually she started inviting people to join us for our weekly dinner.

Elizabeth rode in the car with me when I picked up speakers and visitors and overheard a great many uplifting conversations. Gradually, she became part of the family. As time passed, Elizabeth confided in me how she had been sexually abused. By this time Elizabeth felt free to begin telling me some of her painful experiences. I think she revealed the most to me while we were working side by side in my kitchen, elbow deep in dishwater or surrounded by chopped vegetables.

When she was eighteen, Elizabeth wrote this poem:

Scared of What?
My heart was dark,
    a narrow hole.
All but for a light
    that shone so bright,
        in my soul.

I was scared, but scared of what?

I tried to run,
    but could not walk.

I tried to yell,
>   but could not talk.

I was scared, but scared of what?

I was praying
>   that I might find.
Someone that would love me,
>   in my own mind.
I did not know
>   how to show
all of the feelings
>   that were to grow.

I was scared, but scared of what?

Then you came
>   and took me away.
Just to show me
>   where to stay.

You were so kind,
>   understanding, and fine to me.
I couldn't figure out
>   why this would be.

I was scared, but scared of what?

You let me see
>   the inside of me
>   that wanted to be free.
You showed me
>   so much more.
You made me feel
>   like I could soar.

You came one day
>   and explained to me.

That there was a power
    that created you and me.

I was scared, but scared of what?

You said that God
    was so kind.
That He loved me
    all of the time.

You went on to say that
    "God so loved the world
        that He gave
            His only begotten Son
                for all who believed
                    in Him should not die,
                        but have everlasting life."

John 3:16

I wasn't scared.
    Was scared no more.

Thank You,

Elizabeth

Through our weaknesses, while we are living our everyday lives, God can make us available to reach the Elizabeths and Kathys of this world. Hospitality is a ministry of encouragement. When we are willing to open our homes, our kitchens, our living rooms, and most of all our hearts to others, God can make exciting things happen.

I lost touch with Elizabeth when she turned eighteen, but I heard from her eight years after that. Since then Elizabeth and I have stayed in touch. Today she is married, has two children, and is active in her church. Elizabeth is learning to be an encourager to others. I am grateful that the Lord used my simple attempt at hospitality to help Elizabeth grow closer to Him.

STORIES FROM THE FRONT

Recently I finally got around to inviting a couple from our home church over for Sunday lunch. Sandy and Mike are young college graduates with promising careers and an adorable new baby. They are busy people and had not yet gotten involved in our church. I was ashamed to discover that although they'd been members of our church for nearly three years, our offer was the first personal invitation they had received from anyone in our congregation. They were eager to become actively involved, but no one had told them where they could serve or had made them feel needed.

I don't think Sandy and Mike are an exceptional case in most of our churches. If only a few church families opened their homes to visitors and new members, we would see a remarkable increase in Christian fellowship and growth in our country.

Last week my good friend Amy called and asked if she could stop by. We turned a quilt, sat in the hot tub, and spent a relaxing evening in light conversation. I had planned to complete several projects that evening, but it was a small sacrifice to spend the evening with my friend. I enjoyed her company.

Amy called the next day to thank me for spending the evening with her. "I didn't say anything last night," she told me, "but yesterday was the worst day of my entire life. I was ready to end it all. Thank you for being there to encourage me when I most needed it." Amy reminded me that we can be an encouragement to others through hospitality even when we don't realize it.

Linda, a preschool teacher, was having trouble with her car. A student's parents loaned her their second car for a week (note this practical form of encouragement). Later, Linda thanked the family of five by serving them a spaghetti dinner, salad, and jello in her tiny apartment. The kids ate at TV trays, and the three adults squeezed around a card table. The children thought it was a great adventure, and a budding friendship took root.

Months later, when the mother was confined to bed after a spinal tap, Linda brought her hospitality to them. First she put together the brownie mix she'd brought with her. While the brownies were baking, filling the house with a delicious aroma, she painted the mother's nails. Then she took the brownies out of the oven, rounded up the three children, and went out for ice cream cones to give Mom an interlude of quiet rest.

Linda knew how to practice hospitality, and it didn't require a large home, a family of her own, or gourmet cuisine.

KEEPING THE RIGHT PERSPECTIVE

The purpose of hospitality does not end with serving someone a cold drink or a hot meal. To practice biblical hospitality, our purpose must be to encourage others. Listen to this helpful insight on the nature of encouragement:

> Every Christian, regardless of gift or training, is called upon to encourage his brothers and sisters. Whatever the direction in which our particular congregation is moving, church life will include spending time in the presence of other Christians. And when we meet together as God's people, we

are to encourage one another, to say and do things that stimulate others to a deeper appreciation of Christ and to stronger commitment to our relationship with Him and with each other.[1]

Even when we make encouragement our goal, however, we cannot control our success. The most we can do is be faithful to our purpose by offering practical gifts of hospitality, and pray that our actions have an encouraging effect. It's so important to keep the right perspective—otherwise, we can feel discouraged or overwhelmed when we just don't seem to be able to do enough.

I have found it helpful to use Larry's distinction between *goals* and *desires* to maintain a clear perspective on what I can and cannot control when I offer hospitality:

A *goal* may be defined as a purpose to which a person is unalterably committed. He assumes unconditional responsibility for a goal, and it can be achieved if he is willing to work at it.

A *desire* may be defined as something wanted that cannot be obtained without the cooperation of another person. It is an objective for which a person can assume no responsibility, because it is beyond his control. Reaching a desire must never become the motivating purpose behind behavior, because then a person is assuming responsibility for something he cannot fulfill on his own.[2]

We are better able to offer truly biblical hospitality when we keep our goals separate from our desires. Our *goal* can be to offer a good meal and friendship to visitors at our church; our *desire* is that they feel encouraged and welcomed and visit our church again. Our *goal* can be to organize and plan a party for families in our neighborhood; our *desire* is that we help some of these people grow closer to the Lord. Our *goal* can be to have an organized, creative party for our child's birthday; our *desire* is that everyone have a happy time. We can better relax and concentrate on offering encouragement to others through hospitality if we set our goals according to what we can control and assign the rest to "desires." Then we should *pray for our desires and work for our goals.*

When I am preparing food for company, I work to make sure I am putting forth my best effort. While I am working, I pray that God will use the hospitality for His good pleasure. This really helps me relax and enjoy what I am doing.

Another way I try to keep from worrying is to imagine the worst thing that can happen and decide in advance how I will deal with that possibility. For example: *If the dessert does not turn out, I will serve ice cream. If the roast is not done when I cut it, I'll cook it in the microwave for a few extra moments. If no one shows up, we will enjoy a nice family meal.*

Our goals in practicing hospitality should focus not simply on our physical preparations, though these are important, but on our ultimate purpose: to offer Christ's love to others.

A song by Babbie Mason perfectly describes the ultimate goal of hospitality:

Show Me How to Love
You didn't have to leave the glory of Heaven,
but you became a simple man.
You didn't have to serve the poor and afflicted,
but you touched and healed their brokenness.

No greater love has been given.
You became the ultimate sacrifice.
Create in me the heart of a servant.
Let this be my soul's desire.

Show me how to love
in the true meaning of the word.
Teach me to sacrifice
expecting nothing in return.
I want to give my life away
becoming more like you each and every day.
My words are not enough.
Show me how to love.

I saw a bruised and battered woman
with her hungry children on the street.
Then I heard you ask in that still voice,
"What have you done for the least of these?"
Lord, consume me with a burning fire
that melts away my complacency.
Then let me be moved with love and compassion.
Then someone will find the way in me.

Open up my eyes that I might really see
more and more of you and less of me.
By loving the unlovable
and touching the untouchable
Let my actions speak louder than my words.[3]

The next few chapters of this book will share ideas
for simple activities, meals, decorations, and parties. My
goal is to give you practical tips to increase your confidence; my desire is that you relax and enjoy practicing
hospitality.

NOTES
1. Lawrence J. Crabb, Jr., and Dan B. Allender, *Encouragement: The Key to Caring* (Grand Rapids: Zondervan, Pyranee Books, 1984), page 15.
2. Crabb and Allender, page 52.
3. Babbie Mason, "Show Me How to Love," *Carry On*, © 1988 Word Music (a division of Word, Inc.). All rights reserved, international copyright secured. Used by permission.

Chapter 2

❖

EASY AS PIE . . .
OR EVEN EASIER!

W hen I was growing up, my mother painstakingly
showed me how to make lemon meringue pie
from scratch. After mixing the shortening and flour, we
rolled out the dough, and I pieced it back together when it
fell apart. By this time the entire kitchen would be dusted
with flour. We squeezed lemons and cooked the filling,
and I learned how to keep the mixture from scorching
and sticking. Next, we whipped the egg whites, and
my mother showed me how to swirl them just right and
brown them in the oven without burning the pretty tips.

After many tries—with results ranging from crusts
that fell apart to burnt meringue—I finally mastered the
art of making a lemon meringue pie. This became my
personal contribution whenever we had special company.
Even though I was young, I worked to perfect this skill
so I could share a little of myself to show our guests they
were important.

The hard work and practice of making pies is the
first thing I think of when I hear the expression "easy as
pie"—*not* my idea of easy. In all honesty, I rarely have
time to make lemon meringue pies from scratch these
days, so "easy as pie" has taken on a different meaning

for me. The purpose of this chapter is to give you ideas of ways to encourage others through hospitality that are truly as easy as pie or even easier.

CREATING A CLIMATE

We offer hospitality when we create a loving climate in which others can bloom. The Bible records many examples of this kind of ministry:

- ◆ Mary, Martha, and Lazarus opened their home to Jesus to feed Him and give Him a comfortable place as a base from which to conduct His teaching ministry.
- ◆ When Jesus healed Peter's mother-in-law, her first act was to get up and serve her guests (Mark 1:29-31).
- ◆ Simon the leper, Zacchaeus, Levi, and many others opened their homes to Jesus.
- ◆ The early Church believers met together in each other's homes to pray, praise, worship, fellowship, and eat together. Perhaps the comfortable · environment of a home or the relaxed atmosphere around a meal helped make people receptive to the teaching of the Lord.

In addition to providing examples of hospitality, Scripture gives us specific instructions to practice this kind of loving care for others. In his letters to Timothy and Titus, Paul listed it as a necessary qualification of an elder of the church. He combined encouragement and hospitality as important Christian traits in Titus 1:8-9: "He must be hospitable, one who loves what is good, who is self-controlled, upright, holy and disciplined. He must hold firmly to the trustworthy message as it has been taught, so that he can encourage others by sound doctrine."

Paul's instructions in Romans 12:9-13 emphasize that this ministry of love in action belongs not just to elders, but should be a trademark of all believers:

> Love must be sincere. Hate what is evil; cling to what is good. Be devoted to one another in brotherly love. Honor one another above yourselves. Never be lacking in zeal, but keep your spiritual fervor, serving the Lord. Be joyful in hope, patient in affliction, faithful in prayer. Share with God's people who are in need. Practice hospitality.

Webster defines hospitality as "the reception and entertainment of guests or strangers with liberality and kindness." Notice the key words: *liberality* and *kindness*. Liberality means giving generously; kindness means treating gently and considerately. Doesn't this definition of hospitality create a picture of a loving, encouraging atmosphere? Peter reminds us that this should always be a glad, not a grudging, ministry: "Offer hospitality to one another without grumbling" (1 Peter 4:9).

GIVING OF OURSELVES

The emphasis in our practice of hospitality should be on how we give of ourselves to minister to others—not on how we perform to entertain others. The Bible commands us to carry out this ministry; it does not set up requirements for housing or meals. We do not need a large, beautifully decorated, immaculately tidy house in order to invite others into our home. "Breaking bread" with others does not require serving filet mignon or lobster tails. The issue is not spending money, but spending our time — not giving things, but giving ourselves.

"But the last thing I feel up to doing is sacrificing more of my time!" you protest. "On the schedule I keep, there's not much left of me to give to anyone else, never mind my family! I'm barely holding things together as it is. How can I fit in anything else? I just don't have the energy or creativity to come up with creative ways to minister to others."

If you are overwhelmed at the prospect of offering hospitality, you're not alone. We all feel the pull of overscheduled days and hectic weeks. Relax! Offering hospitality can be as easy as delivering a homebaked pie to a coworker's desk . . . or buying a discouraged friend a cup of coffee . . . or dropping a funny card in the mail.

Even the most harried woman can give of herself in small but effective ways. The key is to *care* for others, to show kindness, to let others see a bit of Christ shining through. There are no hospitality "rules" that apply to every person. As a matter of fact, our unique ways of practicing hospitality — our "personal touch" — is what makes our different ministries so effective!

FOCUS ON THE GIVING RATHER THAN THE GIFT

If you would like to be more active in offering hospitality, I would encourage you to begin in a small, simple fashion. Don't start off by hosting your parent's fiftieth wedding anniversary celebration for one hundred people. That would overwhelm even the most experienced hostess! Begin by offering hospitality that requires little preparation, yet gives of yourself.

I'll never forget an especially difficult day I was having one September. I was up to my ears in work and so far behind schedule I thought I'd never be caught up again. I groaned when the doorbell rang, hating the thought of another interruption. When I opened the door, there stood Ann. She had stopped at a garage sale and picked up a cute, chipped mug for ten cents, drove back to her home and filled it with golden chrysanthemums she cut from her garden, and then brought it by as a gift for me. Her investment of a dime, a few flowers, and fifteen minutes really uplifted me. She didn't stay to chat, because she was having a busy day as well, but her kind action really made a difference in my attitude.

One day Kathy called me while I was feeling very discouraged. I didn't tell her anything about the concerns I was having, but she evidently heard the strain in my voice. She surprised me later that same day with a helium-filled balloon that said, "Don't let the turkeys get you down" and a single orange rose. She didn't even know what was wrong, and she didn't ask — what mattered was that she offered me encouragement.

LOW-DEMAND HOSPITALITY

There are many low-demand ways you can offer hospitality. Pick up a coffeecake and invite a friend over for coffee or tea and a visit. Take someone to a nice restaurant in the middle of the afternoon or after supper for a cup of coffee or a soda. Invite friends over *after* lunch or supper for an informal time of sharing.

Some of our closest friends have extremely busy schedules. It seems impossible to plan ahead for an evening to get together. If we suddenly discover we have a free evening, we may call them on the spur of the moment and ask them to pick up pizzas and soft drinks on their way over for a casual evening. Often we have found that impromptu evenings have ministered the most, not only to our guests but to our family as well.

The atmosphere you provide is much more important than the type of refreshment you serve, the games you plan, or the decorations you use. Try to have comfortable seating with chairs that face each other in an informal circle so guests can see and hear each other. If you have tables or trays, place them within easy reach so your guests have a place to set their drink while they're visiting.

Unless you have specifically gotten together to watch a game or special program, turn off the television. It is difficult to carry on a conversation when you're competing with a full-color, action-packed commercial.

If your home is not "kid proofed," you do not necessarily have to move the furniture when you invite someone over with children. On the other hand, you don't want to spend the entire time jumping around nervously, snatching fragile items out of their hands or blurting out, "Don't touch!" If your visitor brings her crawling baby or active toddler, you may want to move plants or delicate breakables out of reach. Supply young guests with a book or two or even a collection of plastic cups and spoons from your kitchen, and the grownups will feel more relaxed while the youngsters enjoy themselves. I know several older people who keep a small shoe box or a corner of their closet for a few toys, plastic blocks, crayons, and paper to accommodate visiting children. It is a small effort, but greatly appreciated.

I don't insist that my parties have to be a success, nor do I demand that *I* have to make everything happen. Right after we moved to Colorado, I had a "hen party." I really like those times when I can invite over my single and married female friends who may need a break in their schedules. Our transition was a very busy time for me, so I had little time for preparations, but it was also a golden opportunity for this group of women to get together. I had to attend a meeting the evening my friends came, so I supplied them with a few good videotapes for entertainment while I was gone. Each woman brought her own sleeping bag and a topping for a baked potato. My entire contribution for our meal was to put the potatoes in the oven. We ended up with all kinds of toppings—shredded cheese, taco sauce, croutons, bacon bits, etc.—for a feast that required no preparation and little expense.

Sometimes the best opportunities for practicing hospitality do not come at the most convenient times. Martha, who is a working mother of three, told me about an especially busy weekend: "Vacation Bible School begins on Monday, and I have been working on the curriculum. My twentieth class reunion is Saturday night, and we are having a houseguest for the weekend. On Sunday, after I teach Sunday school and have the VBS teacher dedication, we are having twenty-five to thirty people for brunch to meet our guest. Then friends are arriving to go with us to our son's last play performance. They are spending the night, and when they leave Monday morning, I'm back at work, finishing up the final loose ends for VBS on my lunch hour."

This woman is not a superwoman. Martha is a normal Christian woman trying to do her best who is not always able to schedule important events to happen at convenient times. How did she cope with the whirlwind weekend?

First, Martha enlisted help. She really had no control over the timing of her houseguest's visit, so she asked another couple to take the guest out for the evening while she attended her class reunion. She asked someone else to make an egg casserole for the Sunday brunch, while she prepared fruit and muffins ahead of time. Before church on Sunday, she took care of last minute details. While the lunch guests were leaving as her evening guests arrived, she put a casserole she had previously prepared in the oven.

When the weekend was over, Martha told me, "I thought the schedule for the weekend was impossible. But I just did my best and trusted the results to the Lord." I know we all have experienced times when we knew we were overcommitted and depended on the Lord's strength to get us through. It is exciting to see what can happen.

Then there are times when we are just too tired and emotionally depleted to be able to entertain at all. This occurred for us shortly after our move, when we were really looking forward to having friends spend a few days with us. But instead of happily preparing for our guests, I found myself surrounded by carpenters and painters in our new home. Nothing was going as planned. I called Larry and told him I was ready to collapse in five minutes. He replied, "Get out of the house in four!" We decided it would be best for all of us if we were to call and *un*-invite our guests. I knew there would be other times when we would be better able to provide our friends with our companionship, and I knew they would understand. Sometimes it's simply better to reschedule when we're overcommitted. Don't be afraid to make those changes when you need to.

LOOK FOR THE EVERYDAY OPPORTUNITIES

Another way to be more active in encouraging others is to take advantage of the opportunities that arise out of your day-to-day activities. If you sign up to bake cookies for a church program, why not ask a friend to come over and visit with you while you bake? Ask a friend to help you make strawberry jam or freeze peaches. My mother and I always enjoyed our best discussions while we were canning green beans or freezing corn. Women used to share hospitality while they made quilts together; perhaps we are missing golden opportunities when we do so much of our work alone.

Why not invite a new neighbor to meet you at the park for an hour? Ask someone to come over and help you make a large puzzle or sort through old photographs. If you would like to invite a new acquaintance but aren't sure you have enough in common to keep a conversation going, ask another friend or two to join you as well.

Try not to miss the Holy Spirit's nudgings. I almost never drop in on friends unannounced, especially during the day. However, there was a day last fall when I was running errands and found myself driving near a friend's neighborhood. I knew Claudia might be home at that particular time. I really didn't have time to "spare," but I definitely felt something telling me to stop by her house. I drove a few blocks out of my way and rang her doorbell.

When Claudia came to the door, she hugged me and then began to cry. She had just hung up the telephone after learning that a close friend and her three children had all been killed in a car accident. I could do nothing more than listen, cry with her, and promise to pray, but I am convinced the Lord used me to encourage her at that precise moment. My small investment of ten minutes of time and a few tears was helpful to her and bonded us closer together in a spirit of Christian love.

We all have different personalities and styles. Don't try to convince everyone to entertain as you do or expect them to fit into your style of entertaining. Some folks are more quiet and reflective, more consumed by work and other things. For them, thoughtful words, gestures, notes, and listening and asking questions of others is being hospitable. Here are a few ideas.

A Kind Word

One Sunday Larry went into a Sunday school class really feeling low. He thought to himself, *No one ever thinks the psychologist has a difficult day.* He was pleasantly surprised when a young man in the class noticed his state. All he said was, "Hey, you look really tired," but his *noticing* encouraged Larry. Just a kind word or concerned comment can build someone up.

A Thoughtful Gesture

Everyone can be thoughtful, and even a small gesture can have a positive impact. When we moved to Denver, Dan, Larry's associate, stopped in while I was in the midst of carpenters, painters, and unpacking. I felt frazzled! I sat down on the one clear spot on the livingroom sofa, and Dan pinched my toes. I moaned in pain, suddenly realizing what a toll the move had taken on my tired feet. Dan took off my shoes and rubbed my feet. What a tangible gesture of encouragement!

When you see a family traipsing into church five minutes late with a string of kids in tow, get out of your seat and help the kids find junior church or hand them a hymnbook or a program. Small gestures can have big results.

Notes

When Judy was living with us in Indiana, she was having a trying time as she sought the Lord's will for a career change. Larry put encouragement into action. When Judy got up one morning, she found a note outside her bedroom door that said, "Good morning, Judy, this is the first of several instructions. To get the next instruction go to the fireplace mantle."

On the mantle, the short note read, "Go to the coffee pot." The next series of notes ended with, "Go to your computer."

The final note Judy found on her computer read, "If you were willing and had the energy to follow these ridiculous notes all over the house, you are no longer depressed. Now send out five resumes today."

A Simple Gift
Never underestimate the value of a small gift. A friend once mentioned to me that she had been looking everywhere for a teal turtleneck to go with a special outfit. When I was shopping a few days later, I happened to see a teal turtleneck on sale for three dollars. I immediately thought of Nancy and bought the shirt for her. The gift was not as important as the fact that I heard what she said and remembered. It means a lot to people to know that you paid attention, heard what they said, and think about what they like.

I love to hear the story of Al's flamingos. Al and Jerry both hate pink plastic flamingos, especially the yard-ornament kind. Al spotted some gaudy flamingos at a yard sale and one evening placed them in Jerry's yard. For several years, the flamingos were smuggled back and forth.

Then for Al's birthday, Jerry and his wife bought him an inexpensive flamingo mobile, which he hung in his office. This was followed by a flamingo towel, poster, magnet, and pencil. The funniest part of their exchange occurred on a trip to the zoo. Al's young son was so excited to see the real flamingos that he shouted, "Dad, Dad, there's your favorite bird!" The flamingo joke had gone on for such a long time that they had actually started to like them!

Our son Kenny and his friend Doug Lemon give each other crazy gifts. They have exchanged "lemon and crab" or "crab and lemon" shirts. One of the funniest gifts Kenny came up with was a huge photo poster of himself playing tennis on which he had neatly printed "Ken Crabb is my hero." The last I heard, the poster was still hanging in Doug's room. Doug volleyed back by giving Ken a T-shirt with a computer picture of himself. Simple gifts—whether nice or fun and crazy—say "I care."

Follow-Up

When someone makes a comment to you, listen and then respond in a way that invites further conversation. For example, if someone says she has seen a good movie, instead of saying, "I did, too," ask her another question. "What did you like best about it?" invites her into a conversation with you.

If a person comments, "I am really feeling down, and my job is bugging me," don't simply toss it off by saying you will pray for her. "How is it bothering you?" or "Are your coworkers difficult to work with?" are questions that will draw her out and let her know that you really are interested in how she feels and what she is experiencing.

Remember Younger People

Dawn was surprised that one of the girls in the youth group she and her husband helped out with always wanted to ride in their car on the way to youth activities. "All of the people who were driving were friendly people, and most of them had nicer cars," Dawn told me. "I wasn't sure why Julie always wanted to be with us.

"Finally Julie said to us, 'You know why I like riding with you? You talk to *us*. You and Bob don't just talk to each other or talk down to us.'" Young people especially can tell when you are genuinely interested in them and what they have to say.

The little girl next door to us would come over every time I worked in the yard. She would hand me the bulbs as I planted or my tools as I needed them and chat away. She always told me how much she hated dogs—especially our big dog, Ginger. I did not say a word about Ginger's redeeming qualities. By the end of the year she was petting Ginger. Watching her enjoy our big dog reminded me of the impact we can have on others' lives in important ways without ever saying a word, just by our actions and example.

As a child, I visited two neighbors regularly. Neither of them had any daughters, so I would drop by and help them dust, and they would talk with me and make me feel special. Their attitude of encouragement made me think I had the best stroke with a dust cloth of anyone in town.

Feeling squeezed? Don't be afraid to keep hospitality simple. Buy ice cream, meet a friend at the sandwich shop down the street, offer to bring over lunch—then pick up egg rolls and tea bags. Focus on people, not preparations. In the Lord's hands, a few loaves and fishes go a long way.

Chapter 3

❖

SURPRISE COMPANY!

I was right in the middle of a project that I was hurrying to finish. Fabric and banner materials were scattered all over the kitchen. The kids were playing, leaving papers, sleeping bags, and toys helter skelter around the house. The beds were unmade, and pajamas were laying right where they had been tossed earlier that morning. I was determined to finish this banner before another Easter had passed, but it meant letting everything else slide for a day or two.

Naturally, at the height of the frenzy, the doorbell rang. I groaned as I took pins out of my mouth, dropped a pile of felt onto the counter, and went to answer the door.

Standing there was a friend I hadn't seen in fifteen years! How I longed to impress her with a tidy home, freshly baked cookies, and immaculately groomed children. I comforted myself that I was experiencing a natural reaction, but I chided myself on my pride, which I struggled to suppress as I hugged my friend.

"Come in," I said cheerfully. Inwardly, I wondered how I could scoot the toys out of the way with my foot before she noticed them.

"It's so good to see you!" I honestly could say as I breathed a prayer that the Lord would give me the right words of encouragement.

I knew Christine had never given her life to Jesus. She knew I was a Christian. What had prompted her to stop by after all these years? How could the Lord use this moment to help her find her way closer to Him? Then it hit me that her need was not to find me in a perfectly decorated, sparkling clean home with fresh bread baking in the oven and model children practicing the piano. She needed a few moments of intimacy, a chance to share memories and gain encouragement. She needed someone who cared enough to give her a little time and a listening ear.

I put on a pot of tea, and we briefly caught up on the past few years of our lives. She asked me about my family and I learned more about her life as I made peanut butter sandwiches for the boys' lunch and got the younger one ready for kindergarten. I prayed that the Lord would give me the right words to encourage her. I had to trust Him, because I didn't have answers to her questions.

Chris told me about her problems with drinking and her resolve to quit. I responded that I was certain that if I hadn't given Christ first place in my life, I too would be mired in problems.

Being a Christian doesn't mean I no longer have difficulties or that I have become perfect, but I do have a God who loves me and sees me through every situation.

My pride made me shudder again as she insisted on taking pictures of us in the messy livingroom before she left. Again I asked the Lord for the words to say as we gave each other a big hug before she climbed into her Jeep to drive away.

"I hope you find what you are looking for," I told

her. "I will be praying for you." I really was sincere as I told her I would pray for her.

My pride suffered still more as I delivered my son to kindergarten—late again! "The Lord understands, even if the teacher doesn't," I tried to encourage myself. I continued to pray for Chris throughout the day.

REMEMBERING THE ONE THING NEEDED

I do pray that God will use those few moments to make an impact on Chris that will someday bring her to Him as His child. I have to be content to sow the seeds and trust Him to provide the water and sun.

Chris's surprise visit reminded me of several important points the Lord has been teaching me. I love the story of Mary and Martha from Luke 10:38-41—but I have to admit, I usually sympathize with Martha. I would be severely provoked if while I were scurrying about, trying to put a meal on the table for a large group, everyone else sat comfortably in the livingroom watching television or visiting. I would echo Martha's exasperated complaint: "Lord, don't you care that my sister has left me to do the work by myself? Tell her to help me!"

I must let myself hear Jesus' reply as if He had said it directly to me: "Martha, Martha, you are worried and upset about many things, but only one thing is needed. Mary has chosen what is better, and it will not be taken away from her."

I can almost feel the compassion in Jesus' voice as He gently chides Martha when He speaks her name. I try to hear His words in my ear each time I get worried and upset about preparations I am making. Only one thing is needed. I must remember to make my top priority giving the Lord's encouragement. I must not be consumed by how my own feeble efforts will be perceived: the way my home looks, the way the food tastes, or even if I have any type of refreshment to offer.

Though the Lord is still working on my pride and helping me to learn to relax and keep the most important thing in mind—practicing *encouragement,* not just "hospitality"—I have also tried to gather as much ammunition as possible to be prepared for making the most of every opportunity.

Here are the points I try to remember:

1. Concentrate on *people,* not *preparations.*
2. Keep supplies on hand for putting together one impromptu meal.
3. Have some type of small refreshment on hand: a flavored tea or coffee, cheese and crackers, or cookie dough for quick preparation.
4. Keep my sense of humor and lose my sense of pride. (A few years from now, will guests really remember if the bathroom mirror was spotted when they dropped by?)

IDEAS FOR STAYING PREPARED

Caryl is the best discipler I've ever had in showing me how to offer hospitality. Her husband was transferred from the pastorate to his denomination's national headquarters. Caryl has two children and a job in a medical lab. Joe never knew when past acquaintances might visit the headquarters. He didn't want to miss the chance to fellowship with old friends, so he wasn't able to give Caryl much notice if he invited them home for supper at the last minute.

Caryl stayed prepared. She always kept a jar of spaghetti sauce and a box of pasta in the cupboard, some flavored coffee, and her special pineapple slush and a package of ground beef in the freezer. While she browned the beef and boiled the noodles, she set the table, spooned the slush into fruit dishes as an appetizer, and mixed up a chocolate cake to bake while they ate dinner.

Caryl had several foolproof emergency menus that allowed her to spend as much time as possible visiting with her guests and the least amount of time in the kitchen. She also confessed that if she didn't have time to vacuum, she'd dim the lights and set out candles, and simmer potpourri in the bathroom to make the house smell fresh. Another clever idea Caryl had for filling the house with fragrance was to brown some cinnamon in a pan on the stove for a few minutes. She said that came in handy when they were trying to sell their house and only had moments to tidy up before potential buyers barged in.

Later in this chapter you'll find some recipes for Caryl's favorite emergency rations. Her pineapple slush could serve as an appetizer, fruit salad, or dessert. Her chocolate cake topped with chocolate chips and nuts is delicious and smells great while baking during dinner. It takes only two minutes to mix up a yogurt pie if you have a graham cracker crust on hand, and only ten minutes more if you mix a ground nut or cookie crust to pat into the pie plate before filling. I try to keep either an empty graham cracker crust in the pantry or ground nuts or cookies in the freezer to make a fast pie.

I'll never forget the time Caryl had the main course for a progressive dinner for all the couples in our church. She moved the furniture, brought in card tables and extra chairs, and covered every table with a tablecloth.

She set each table with china place settings (borrowed from several families in the church) and candles. Several people brought spaghetti sauce or browned meat, which she then mixed together into one big pot to keep warm in the kitchen. A salad, breadsticks, and beverages rounded out the hearty meal, which helped develop friendships throughout the congregation.

The most important lesson I learned from Caryl was not her special tips for entertaining, but her attitude of encouragement. She always kept her emphasis on the *people* she was trying to encourage, not just the *preparations*.

Caryl and Joe now live in Seattle, Washington, where they minister through an inner-city church. In the few years they've been there, they have enlarged their ministry of hospitality. They open their home to people of all nationalities who live with them as they struggle to learn English and find a job in a new country. Together they share meals and enjoy fellowship with the congregation.

Caryl and Joe continue to extend their practice of hospitality by encouraging and discipling others who are now giving themselves in this ministry.

My friend Jean is another good example of someone who stays prepared to show hospitality. She is married to a gregarious businessman who often spontaneously brings guests home for dinner. Jean always keeps chicken kiev and broccoli in the freezer, and a box of seasoned rice and a brownie mix in the cupboard. While the chicken bakes and the broccoli and rice boil on the stove, she mixes up the brownie mix and sets the table. Jean slides the brownies into the oven when she takes out the chicken and enjoys a meal with her guests. As they finish eating, the smell of warm chocolate fills the house. In time for dessert, the brownies are still warm. Jean tops them with ice cream and fudge sauce or with whipped topping and maraschino cherries.

Jean has also learned to simplify preparations so she can concentrate on encouraging others.

I always keep a canned ham in the pantry for emergency menus. I can bake the ham with pineapple or apple rings, or serve with applesauce. A canned vegetable or fresh salad, packaged potato side dish or rolls, and a dessert can be prepared quickly without much fuss. I often get the ham sliced at the grocery store and freeze it in packages of six to eight slices. I can grill the ham on the barbecue with sauce and serve with fries, baked beans, and deli potato salad.

One delicious item to keep in the freezer is balls of homemade chocolate chip cookie dough. Whenever I have surprise guests, if even just for a cup of coffee or tea, I can stick a pan of cookie dough in the oven within minutes of their arrival. I believe part of practicing encouragement means making my friends feel special. If eating a cookie warm from the oven makes my guests feel special, that helps me encourage them.

My home-frozen peaches have become a reliable emergency menu ration. My family has become hooked on these peeled, sliced, and packed fresh peaches in light syrup, which are tucked away in the freezer for winter enjoyment. I can mix them with other frozen fruit for an appetizer or fruit side dish or spoon them over ice cream for dessert.

For a quick and attractive summer fruit salad, I cut and cube a melon and any other fresh fruit and mix it together with a can of cherry or peach pie filling.

Another quick salad that guests enjoy is prepared by draining a can of mandarin oranges and placing the orange sections and sliced almonds on lettuce, then topping with a sweet dressing such as poppy seed or mayonnaise mixed with honey.

A store-bought angel food cake provides a quick dessert. After slicing it, top it with strawberries or strawberry jam, vanilla pudding, whipped topping, and sliced almonds—or any type of fruit, pudding, or ice cream. Packaged cookies can be substituted for the cake.

Three reliable impromptu snacks are popcorn, ice cream (I like to keep at least one topping on hand), and pizza. Most communities have an outlet where you can buy ready-made pizza crusts. This is a new item in the dairy section of most grocery stores. I keep shredded mozzarella cheese and sliced pepperoni in the freezer and usually have cans of black olives, pizza sauce, and mushrooms in the pantry. A fresh piece of sausage and an onion or green pepper completes our "gourmet" pizzas.

The nice thing about pizza is that you can use a variety of toppings—whatever you have on the shelf. Pizzas can be made with any type of meat—ground beef or sausage, salami, even tuna or shrimp—and any type of vegetable. The only three requirements are the crust (or English muffins), sauce (ketchup or tomato sauce will work with oregano added), and cheese (even cheddar and swiss). Your guests can help you toss on the toppings while you visit—even young guests enjoy joining in. And pizza can be eaten anywhere, whether there is space at a table or not.

My homemade pizza came in very handy when we hosted students from a college singing group that was performing at our church. We brought home for the night four of the tallest young men I have ever seen who, though they had eaten before performing, appeared to be starving. I was eight-and-a-half months pregnant and tried to act nonchalant while experiencing bouts of false labor as I made pizza after pizza to fill their hollow legs.

My older son was still young and thoroughly enjoyed watching these Christian young people in action. One moment will be forever etched in my mind: As I doubled over with a contraction, the boys' faces contorted in horror. For a brief moment, I think they were afraid they were going to witness the birth of a baby. We still laugh over that memory.

My personal favorite emergency dessert is frozen chocolate pie. It takes only minutes to fix and stays fresh in the freezer for weeks. I also like to put peppermint or black raspberry ice cream in a chocolate cookie pie crust and drizzle chocolate sauce over the top.

Sometimes even mistakes can make delicious meals. When we were in England, the flour and sugar were so different it took a bit of adjustment on my part. I put a tray of oatmeal cookies in the oven and later pulled out one solid "cookie." I didn't want to waste the expensive ingredients, so I crumbled up the cookies and put them in the freezer. The next time we had company, I placed the crumbled cookies in dessert dishes and topped them with double cream. Our guests loved the dessert even after I explained it was really a "mistake."

If you are not already in the habit of spontaneous entertaining, it might be worth the time to decide on a sample menu of items that you would like to make and then obtain the ingredients to keep on hand. Just knowing you have something tucked away in the freezer or cupboard makes it much easier to invite someone home on the spur of the moment. Sometimes the richest fellowship occurs in unplanned or unexpected occasions.

However, *don't feel you must provide a meal or entertainment to invite people into your home for fellowship.* There is absolutely nothing wrong with inviting friends over after supper, for a glass of iced tea, or to enjoy take-out food.

The ideas I'm presenting here are to help you plan your own style of practicing hospitality.

A vital part of practicing hospitality is sharing yourself with others in order to encourage them. To do this, you need to relax and be yourself. If "we deliver" pizza is your style, order pizza. If serving filet mignon on your best china is your specialty, go for it. If you are too exhausted to think about food, stop by a delicatessen or take your guests out to eat.

LET YOUR GUESTS PITCH IN

It is often fun to invite your guests to help with the meal. Ask everyone to bring something, or provide the meal and ask your guest to bring the dessert. Why not supply pizza crust and cheese or baked potatoes, and let your guests bring the toppings? Or provide lettuce while your guests bring chopped vegetables and dressings.

Be creative and flexible. Plan a style of entertaining that fits your budget and your lifestyle. The important thing is not to put off practicing hospitality because your home isn't finished or the carpet is threadbare or your cooking skills aren't perfect or your children are too young. It's too easy to think of a hundred-and-one excuses for never inviting anyone over to your home. If you just start somewhere, you'll really enjoy sharing yourself and your home with others. Don't become so involved in the preparation that you forget to enjoy this opportunity to let Christ shine through you.

PLAN-AHEAD MENUS

Here are a few sample menus to give you ideas for what to have on hand for impromptu guests. (Today there is a strong emphasis on serving healthy menus. When in doubt of the diet your guests may prefer, consider broiling a piece of chicken or fish and serving fresh vegetables and fruit.)

Canned ham
Box of scalloped or au gratin potatoes
Canned, fresh, or frozen vegetable
Rolls or bread
Microwave cake

Can or jar of spaghetti sauce
Spaghetti or other noodles
Salad
Frozen pie

Frozen chicken kiev
Frozen broccoli
Packaged rice side dish
Brownies

Pizza crusts
Pizza sauce
Mozzarella cheese
Olives, mushrooms, pepperoni, onions, etc.
Sherbet

Turkey tettrazini or tuna or ham and noodle casserole
Lettuce salad
Fruit salad
Cookies

Tacos (taco shells or corn chips, ground meat, lettuce,
shredded cheese, tomatoes, black olives)
Ice cream

"EMERGENCY" RECIPES

Caryl's Frozen Fruit Slush
This recipe is great for an appetizer, fruit side dish, or topping over ice cream.
Mix together:
> 12 oz. frozen orange juice
> 12 oz. water
> 2 20 oz. cans crushed pineapple (or 1 20 oz. can crushed pineapple and 1 16 oz. drained can of peaches put through the blender — be creative!)
> 6 bananas, diced

Put in containers and freeze.

No-Roll Nut Crust
Melt ½ C. butter or margarine in oven in pie plate. Add 1 C. flour, ¼ C. powdered sugar and ¼ C. finely ground walnuts. You can add a touch of cinnamon. Mix together, pat on sides and bottom of pan, prick well with fork and bake at 400° for 12 minutes.

Caryl's Frozen Yogurt Pie
Mix together 8 oz. of whipped topping with 16 oz. of yogurt. Put mixture in graham cracker crust or a nut or cookie crust and freeze.

Caryl's Quick Chocolate Cake
Cook a small package of chocolate pudding (not instant), following package directions. Add a dry 18¼ oz. box of chocolate cake mix. Place in greased 9" x 12" cake pan and sprinkle 6 oz. of chocolate chips and ½ C. of nuts on top. Bake for 30 min. at 350° while you are eating and serve warm for dessert.

Frozen Chocolate Pie

Blend together with mixer:

    1 C. powdered sugar

    ½ C. softened butter

Blend in:

    6 oz. semisweet chocolate squares, melted and cooled

    1 tsp. vanilla

On high speed, beat in one at a time, mixing well:

    4 eggs

Pour into a baked pie shell (or cracker or cookie crumb crust), cover with plastic wrap and freeze. To serve, add whipped cream and shaved chocolate curls.

Easy Vegetable Salad

Here's an idea for a pretty salad that can be prepared ahead: Slice or dice your favorite garden vegetables, including any of these: carrots, cucumbers, celery, mushrooms, onions, kidney beans, radishes. Cover with a bottle of oil and vinegar-based Italian salad dressing and store in the refrigerator overnight.

Elaine has a wonderful garden every summer that helps supply ingredients for her tasty chili sauce. She makes it each season and freezes it. When she has company, she serves chili with cheese, crackers, and a salad. Her preparations are uncomplicated, but the meal is wonderful.

Elaine's Chili Sauce

Mix together and boil until thick:

    4 quarts fresh tomatoes, peeled and chopped, or

        canned equivalent

    1½ C. green pepper, chopped (2 large)

    2 C. onions, chopped (2 large)

1 to 1½ C. vinegar
1½ C. sugar
1 Tblsp. salt
1 Tblsp. celery seed
1 tsp. ginger
1 tsp. cinnamon
1 tsp. allspice
1 tsp. ground cloves

Freeze sauce. To serve, brown one pound of ground meat, add chili sauce and a 15 oz. can of drained kidney beans, and heat through.

Ham and Cheese Bake

This recipe serves a crowd.
Cook 4-6 oz. of noodles according to package directions.
Gradually blend together:
1 C. milk
8 oz. cream cheese

Heat without boiling until cheese is melted.
Add:
¼ C. parmesan cheese
½ C. celery, diced
¼ C. chopped green pepper
½ tsp. salt
1½ C. sliced ham

Mix together with noodles and place in greased casserole dish. Top with ¼ C. grated parmesan cheese and bake at 350° for 30 minutes.

Years ago, I ran across a menu in a magazine to entertain inexpensively. In 1970, I actually served nineteen people for $1.86. I'm sure ingredients have increased in cost since then, but this cheese souffle recipe is still an economical choice.

Cheese Souffle

Remove crusts (which can be put out for birds) from 12 pieces of day-old bread (wheat or white). Using one 10 oz. can of cheese soup, layer bread in an ungreased casserole, spreading each layer with cheese.
Mix together:

4 beaten eggs
1⅓ C. milk
¼ C. melted butter
⅛ tsp. dry mustard (or a squirt of prepared mustard)

Spoon milk and egg mixture into crevices. Add more milk if necessary. You can store this overnight in the refrigerator and the next day bake at 350° for one hour.

Serve this dish with vegetables, a tossed salad, or fresh fruit. You can top the souffle with a shrimp sauce or a can of shrimp soup or add cooked, crumbled bacon, diced ham, or sausage. It also makes a good side dish with ham if you add pineapple to the mixture before cooking.

Herbed Pork Roast

This recipe is great for lunch following church because it can cook in the crockpot all morning. The night before mix together:

2 C. water
1 tsp. salt
1 tsp. thyme, crumbled
1 tsp. grated lemon peel
1 Tblsp. lemon juice
1 tsp. ground sage

Pour mixture on a 4-7 pound fresh ham or pork roast. Place in a sealed container and marinate overnight. Place in a crockpot in the morning and cook on low for 10-12 hours or high for 4-5 hours. You may also add peeled potatoes under the roast to cook with the meat.

Cherry Cheese Pie

Mix together 8 oz. of cream cheese (softened) with ½ C. sugar and 8 oz. of whipped topping. (You may also add ½-1 tsp. vanilla.) Place in pie shell. Top with one can of cherry pie filling mixed with ¼ tsp. almond extract. Chill.

Party Sandwich Loaf

Take an unsliced loaf of bread and slice horizontally. Spread each layer with a sandwich spread: egg salad, ham salad, etc. Reassemble the loaf of bread. Mix cream cheese with enough milk to make it spreading consistency and spread it over the loaf of bread on all sides, making it look like a package. Wrap in a damp tea towel to store in the refrigerator. When serving, use pimento to make a flower design on the top, tie a ribbon around the "package," or use parsley to make a wreath to decorate the top. Serve buffet style and let each guest cut a slice.

Chapter 4

❖

ADULT PARTIES

W hen we joined our new church at the turn of the year, it didn't take me long to figure out that I would never get to know anyone very well just by passing them in the hallway before or after church. I wasn't even sure which children belonged to whom, and which adults were couples or singles.

There usually isn't a lot of activity in January and February. Out of desperation, I decided to have a Valentine's Day party. I had been to Valentine's parties at two of our previous churches, so I had some experience to get me started.

My first Valentine's party was such a success that we decided it should be an annual event. Not only did I get to know people in our church, but they all got to know each other in a more personal way. We are still chuckling over some of the humorous experiences we shared that evening years ago.

Before everyone arrived, I decorated the house with red and pink crepe paper, candles, and hearts. I asked a few guests to bring either red and white desserts or something chocolate. I made flavored coffees, teas, punch, and decorated a raspberry torte. To counteract the sweets, I served cheese and crackers and a vegetable tray with dip. I purchased pink plastic spoons and forks and pink paper plates and napkins. I kept the preparations simple so I wouldn't be too tired to enjoy our guests.

When each couple arrived, I pinned hearts to their backs with the names of a famous couple. Each couple could ask one yes-or-no question from other guests until they learned the identity of the couple assigned to them. I have learned that having an icebreaker at the beginning of an evening helps people relax and begin conversations much more easily.

After the guests had arrived and identified their famous couple, we all sat in a circle facing each other in our family room. Each couple introduced themselves and shared how they met and where they spent their honeymoon. I still remember a few of the crazy stories we laughed over. I sympathized with the couple who planned a golfing honeymoon and struggled to enjoy their vacation despite the bride's broken leg. Their description of riding in a golf cart with a casted leg protruding from the side had our entire group in stitches.

We also played "The Oldywed Game." The three couples who had been married the longest were the contestants. First the men left the room (they went to the dining room and snacked on the refreshments) while we asked the women three questions: "What is your husband's favorite flavor of ice cream?" "What model of car was the first car you owned?" "What is the oldest item in your refrigerator?" We wrote down the wife's answers. Then the husbands returned, answered the same questions, and those couples with matching answers received points. The women then left the room while the men were asked questions such as, "What is your wife's favorite room in your house?" "Where is her favorite place to eat?" "How much did a postage stamp cost when you were dating?" All the questions were designed to be fun and not embarrassing.

All the contestants received silly prizes. The winners got a box of oatmeal for being the most "mushy," candy bars went to the "sweetest," etc.

Other games that we have enjoyed at Valentine's parties are: "Name that Tune," where you play "oldies but goodies" on the record player and everyone guesses the name of the song or the group that recorded it; "Couple Charades"; and "Pictionary," using a chalkboard and teaming women against men.

After the games, we all enjoyed refreshments and visiting. Conversation was flowing easily by then.

Parties for groups of adults can have many objectives. This chapter will give you ideas for fostering fellowship. Some of the most enjoyable get-togethers we have had began as costume parties. Here are a few ideas.

COSTUME PARTIES

Famous Folks Festival

Invitations encouraged everyone to come dressed as a "Famous Person." Costumes ranged from presidents to Bible characters to famous individuals both real and imagined from current events and books.

A fitting refreshment could be a huge pot of stew cooked over a fire in the yard.

Ad or Fad

During our last "Ad or Fad" party, one guest came dressed as a baseball striker, one couple as the Jolly Green Giant and his tomato, and a masked guest wore red tights under a gold sheet painted to resemble a corn chip package disguised as the Frito Bandito. Anybody or anything that's current is fair game.

It's Not Easy Being Green
"It's not easy being green, except on March 17," read the invitation to a St. Patrick's Day party at a local racquet club. Everyone came dressed in green, ready to play tennis or racquetball.

Decorations included shamrocks and lime green punch.

Mother Goose Party
This costume party really encourages creativity and works well for children and adults. At our last Mother Goose party, one of our guests wore a black cape and red shirt and became Robin Red Breast. A pregnant girl dressed in orange to resemble a pumpkin, and her husband came as Peter. My favorite costume was on a guest who wore cotton long underwear and was covered everywhere with soft wool. He was a lamb. Mistress Mary Quite Contrary looked lovely with lots of ruffles as she carried her watering can.

I had a different centerpiece on each table with a clue to help each person guess where he or she was to sit. I placed an antique clock in the center of one table with the clue as the nursery rhyme "Hickory Dickory Dock, the mouse ran up the _____." Guests repeated nursery rhymes as an icebreaker and to find their seats.

PROGRESSIVE DINNERS

Progressive dinners are a great opportunity for sharing preparations. I have often had guests meet at my home to receive their napkin and toothpick. They can't receive a napkin or toothpick at any other home. This gives everyone a chance to arrive and set off for the next home together. We help everyone get acquainted by playing an icebreaker or two and call the next home just as we are leaving. Progressive dinners do not require seating at each home. One home can offer soup or appetizers; another, salads; a third, the main course; and the last home, the dessert and coffee and tea.

Babes in Foodland
We enjoyed honoring everyone in our church who had been blessed with a new baby in the past year with an unusual progressive dinner. We met at the church and received a menu and itinerary for the evening. The menu read:

Appetizers
Infantile cocktail hot dogs
Cheddar juniors
Juvenile sandwiches
Tiny olives, pickles, onions

Salads
Stuffed cherry tomatoes
Tiny finger jello molds
Strained apples (adult version)
Stuffed eggs
Yucky green stuff (lettuce salad)

Main Course
Baby carrots
Infant Cornish hens
Rattle rice
Juice, strained and clarified

Dessert
Baby-food carrot cake
Tiny blueberry muffins
Baby peanut butter squares
Pat-a-cake pies
Tiny, individual cherry pies with frosting and nuts
Chocolate glazed miniature cream puffs

Icebreakers encouraged everyone to try to discover the middle name of each new baby and the infant who weighed the least at birth. Games at the last home included a memory game with a tray full of baby items presented in full view for one minute, then taken away; a list of scrambled baby words; and a game to guess the name of animal babies. Other games could include remembering the end of nursery rhymes or having a doll-dressing contest for each new father including diapers, undershirts, and sleepers.

Centerpieces could include pink and blue candles and curling ribbon, baby shoes, blocks, or small stuffed animals. Pink and blue napkins can be pinned with new diaper pins, which can be given to the new parents.

A good idea for a baby shower is to give each person one half sheet of pink or blue paper. I make copies of a small, cute illustration of a teddy bear and copy it on each sheet of paper before the shower. Each person then writes a personal message to the honored guest. At the end of the shower, the papers are gathered, punched with two holes, and put together with a ribbon for the guest to save.

Neighborhood Dinners
We once celebrated New Year's Eve with a progressive dinner in our neighborhood in Boca Raton. After going from home to home, we gathered at our church for a

watchnight service to pray in the new year. One of my nonChristian neighbors called me several times the following week to tell me what a great evening she'd had. "Rachael," she kept repeating, "I didn't think anyone could have so much fun without drinking."

When we first moved to that neighborhood, there was about one Christian family on each of the sixteen streets. The first progressive dinner opened the door to other communication, and soon we began our first neighborhood Bible study. We began with one Bible study of six women to study the Gospel of Mark and pray for our neighbors. By the eighth chapter of Mark, there were eight of us and by the end of Mark, sixteen. After a year, our small group of women had multiplied to become twenty-three Bible studies meeting weekly in Boca Raton. That year of Christian growth has always encouraged me to continue this form of encouragement.

SEASONAL PARTIES

Super Bowl Sunday
We enjoy inviting friends over to watch an exciting football game—especially the Super Bowl. When we lived in Florida, I painted an old football helmet white and filled it with orange roses to match our team's colors for a centerpiece. I found a wallpaper border at an outlet store that matched our team and used it for decorations. I strung up a few pennants and left several footballs in the corner of the room. We asked all of our guests to bring along their favorite snack.

Fall Festival
When we moved to Colorado, I invited neighbors over for a Fall Festival. I decorated the drive with luminaries,

using orange paper sacks with candles burning inside. I served warm and cold apple cider and a lot of pumpkin goodies: cookies, pies, and bread. My invitation to the neighbors gave the time, the place, and the why: "So *we* can get to know *you!*"

Family Fall Festivals offer an opportunity for fellowship. A hay ride, a crackling fire to roast hot dogs and marshmallows, relay and sack races, and other types of active games all give families and friends an enjoyable evening. Ask someone to bring a guitar so you can all sing camp songs while riding in the hay wagon. Offer prizes for the best decorated pumpkin. When the pumpkins arrive, place lighted candles in them and use them to help light the yard. Supply hot cider and hot chocolate. Keep the food simple, so it's easier to eat in the dark. A big pot of chili cooking on the fire, chips, and brownies or "S'mores" (chocolate bars and toasted marshmallows sandwiched between graham crackers) always taste great on a chilly fall evening.

One year we couldn't accommodate a real hay ride, so we filled a garden cart with hay and hooked it up to a lawn tractor to give all the tiny tots "hay rides" around the yard. That was a hay ride those little children will never forget.

I usually rent or borrow a videotape children would enjoy, just in case the weather does not cooperate and we end up celebrating inside.

SPECIAL EVENT PARTIES

Bobby Crocker Cook-Off

One of the most entertaining evenings I've ever attended was a Bobby Crocker Cook-Off. The men prepared all the desserts and the women judged them. Prizes were awarded for the best creations, and of course everyone enjoyed eating the entries. Less adventuresome spouses can always bring store-bought cookies or prepare the coffee.

Japanese Party
An oriental-looking sheet to cover the table, egg rolls, and seats on the floor help guests relax and enjoy a Japanese atmosphere. Origami place cards help guests find their place. Chopsticks are optional.

Come as You Are, But Bring Something
Linda was single and had a tiny apartment, but she was determined to encourage fellowship and build bridges between her Christian and nonChristian friends.

One weekend, Linda called several friends: couples and singles from college age to senior citizens. She invited them to come to her house the next evening at 7:00 with a snack item that began with the same letter as their last name. Jim Tinkey brought taco chips, Longs brought lemon drops, Carrs brought chocolate chip cookies. Linda's guests sat on the floor and furniture squeezed together in the small livingroom. There wasn't much room to move around, so Linda passed each snack item around the room and as the guests helped themselves to the unusual assortment, they had to guess who had brought each item. By the time all the snacks were passed, the ice was broken and everyone was beginning to have a wonderful time.

I was interested to note that conversation increased just because we were all together in one room. Some of it was in small pockets and some of it moved across the entire group, but it all flowed at the same time. Because we couldn't move around easily, we all got to know the people we were sitting near, and many new friendships began.

Years later, when Linda was married and had a lovely, large home, she had a party to celebrate obtaining her master's degree. Many of the same people came to congratulate her, and we found ourselves reminiscing about the "Come as You Are" party we had enjoyed a few years earlier. It was only then that we found out about the very next party Linda had thrown—a much smaller one than ours. Linda's husband told us that he had been invited to her apartment and arrived on time, but no one else ever showed up. Linda insists no one else could come, but none of us recalls ever being invited. We all got a kick out of Linda's ingenuity!

Spanning the Generations

I recently attended a party at a Christian day school on the theme, "Reflections . . . Spanning the Generations," intended to encourage interaction among the generations. School students had invited grandparents and grandpersons, older friends of the family and members of the church.

One person announced each part of the program, which began with the children singing a song of appreciation to their guests. This was followed by skits between grandmothers and their grandchildren discussing how things had changed since the grandmother's youth along with values that had remained the same. The grandchildren in each skit gained a new appreciation for their heritage and each learned something new about their parents.

Following the skits, an adult read a sentimental piece, and then a song by Twila Paris entitled "Same Girl" was played from a cassette. The attendees then broke into small groups of combined ages. At each small group, beginning with the youngest member, players took turns drawing and then answering a question. There were questions in three categories: one for children, one for adults, and one for grandpersons. For example, one question might read, "What was Christmas like when you were a child?" (for the grandperson or adult) and "What is your favorite part about Christmas?" (for the child). Questions ranged from favorite hobbies and books, how children thought their grandparents dressed and what school might have been like, followed by the older people recalling what it was really like. One question asked younger persons how they thought they were like their grandparents. Everyone gained a new appreciation for each other.

This type of party is appropriate for any size group and is a unique way to make senior citizens feel important and alive and help young people appreciate and get to know the grandpersons in their lives.

Cookie Exchanges

There were fourteen homes in our neighborhood in Warsaw. A few of the women in the neighborhood and I decided to combine a neighborhood project with our cookie exchange. There was a group home in our neighborhood, so a few of us visited it to see what they might need. The home was very nice but had few frills, so we decided to bring items to decorate it.

At least one member of each family in our neighborhood came to our home to celebrate. Each family contributed three dozen cookies: one dozen for the snack table, one dozen to swap, and one dozen for the group home. They also brought a wrapped gift for the group home. I served egg nog, coffee, tea, and punch.

The purpose of our neighborhood cookie exchange

was not only to foster fellowship among our neighbors and give us a chance to witness to others, but also to reach out in a loving way to the residents of the group home.

A cookie exchange can be organized for any group — neighborhood, work, Bible study, Sunday school class. If you don't already have a special project, put cookies on pretty trays wrapped with plastic and ribbon and deliver them to shut-ins or nursing homes. Around Christmas, it helps the holiday spirit if you sing a few Christmas carols when delivering.

Open House

One of my favorite ways to entertain during the holidays, or when a special friend or returning missionary is visiting locally, is to plan an open house. Invite guests to come any time within specified hours, so more people can attend without your home being too crowded. I fill a table or the kitchen counter with food and beverages and let people help themselves. Weather permitting, I put candles and sand in small decorated sacks to serve as luminaries along the sidewalk and deck.

I try to have several areas for visiting throughout our home with small groups of chairs facing each other to encourage conversation. I occasionally check on the refreshments and circulate to introduce guests to each other and enjoy the company.

For one of her holiday parties, my sister covered small tables with plaid tablecloths and set a small battery-operated lantern on top of each table. The lanterns produced a very warm, friendly atmosphere. Another friend decorated her entire home with a gingerbread theme for a holiday open house. She used cookie cutters and gingerbread houses for decorations.

If you have invited guests from different groups

of friends, consider using name tags. You can purchase standard name tags or cut an appropriate shape out of construction paper. Have a small table with pens and pins so your guests can help themselves to a name tag as they arrive.

Amateur Artist Party

One of my homes had long hallways, which were great fun for having an art party. As guests arrived, they were handed a drawing tablet and given the name of another guest they were to sketch. The "artists" were not to let the subjects know who was drawing them. When all had finished their illustrations, we taped them on the wall up and down the hallway and then tried to identify the person in each sketch.

During the evening, we all had a great time improving our drawing skills. For one game, we held our tablets on top of our heads and drew an object. Another game required us to draw an object as it was being described to us. We had quite a variety of drawings that night.

Game Parties

An informal evening of games can be very entertaining without requiring a lot of work. Place card tables in several areas in your home and put a different game at each table. Try to have a variety of types of games, some using words or letters, others using drawing skills, and a few traditional board games. Give each guest a card assigning them a table number for each round. Every twenty minutes or so, ring a bell and let people fill their plates with snacks before going on to a different table for the next round. (It helps if one player at each table has previously played that particular game, but it's not essential.)

We had several new teachers at our children's school

and used a game night as an opportunity to get to know our teachers and principal. For this game activity, a teacher or principal stayed at the same game table throughout the evening and the parents changed tables for each round. We served popcorn and cold drinks, and parents brought snack items.

Additional Suggestions

These party ideas can be adapted for families within your church congregation, neighborhood, or work sphere. If you are married, remember to invite the single people in your community. Guests lists do not need to be in even numbers. In fact, unless an evening is specifically planned for couples, such as a Valentine's party, it's usually more enjoyable to include a variety of people.

Even when you put "RSVP" on your invitation, you will probably have to check back with your guests. Many people neglect to respond to invitations or forget the date, so a telephone call a few days in advance can be a helpful reminder.

Try keeping a notebook, folder, or index card file with notes on past entertaining. Your entries may include who likes tea, but not coffee; food allergies or dislikes; how many people attended your last party and how much food was served. I keep a list of the games played and the people attending our Valentine's party so I can make sure the ideas are fresh each year. It also helps me to know which foods went well, what ran out, and which food items were left over.

WHAT TO DO WITH YOUR SHY GUESTS

Despite the best ideas, not everyone likes parties. You may have guests who are shy or hang back from some of the activities I've described in this chapter. These folks don't jump into icebreakers with enthusiasm. How can you offer the kind of encouragement your more shy or "serious" guests need while they're in your home?

With shy people especially, don't give the impression that to fit in your home they have to be just like you. Some guests will reluctantly participate with a bit of encouragement—and they'll end up having a great time. Some truly don't like to be pushed and may enjoy quiet conversation.

You may know people who would not feel comfortable as a guest in others' homes—but you can still minister to them.

Loraine always sat in the back seat at church and was quickly out the door at the last Amen. She was terribly shy. My goal was not, however, to get her to sit up front and be friendly. My goal was to greet her at every service without fail, even if I had to run after her. I started sitting in the vicinity where she would sit. I made a point at every service to say, "Hello, Loraine."

Two years later, I started receiving Snoopy cards regularly from Loraine thanking me for my encouragement. I had to turn the cards all the way around to find her name written in tiny letters. After three cards, she wrote me a poem expressing what my talking to her every Sunday had meant. Loraine would not have felt comfortable at any of my parties, but I could offer another type of encouragement that she was willing to receive.

At your parties, be willing to step out of the center of attention. Sit off in the corner and have a quiet conversation with a person who is not that visible. If someone is shy, introduce her to someone else saying, "Judy, this is Karen; she likes knitting, too." Or, "Frank, Brian is also a coach for his son's soccer team. How's your season going?"

I really liked an idea my friend had when she invited us to a party at her home. Before the event, Ann sent everyone who had been invited a short biography sheet of the guests telling who they were, what they did, and something interesting about them. There were no quiet people at this party, because we all felt as if we knew each other before we arrived.

You may not have the time, room, or desire to plan elaborate or even simple parties for your friends, but if you do enjoy having guests in your home, there are things you can do to make them feel welcome. The next chapter will give you practical suggestions for what to do when they arrive.

Chapter 5

❖
_____

THEY'RE HERE —
NOW WHAT?!

Your guests have arrived. Now what do you do? How do you offer hospitality that encourages them?

First, you can show your guests — whether they were expected or have dropped in unannounced — that they are important to you. Do this by really listening to them and making an effort to relax while they're with you.

Try to move beyond words only in your encouragement. It doesn't mean much to say "I'll pray for you" if you really have no intention of ever thinking of this person or her difficulties again. "Those words ought to have awesome power to encourage," writes Larry, "because prayer is our vital link with the Lord. So why do they sometimes not move us? Because words have power only to the degree that they represent meaningful involvement."[1]

THE FIRST WORDS OUT OF YOUR MOUTH

You are showing your personal involvement by offering hospitality. It is important to remember that the second step has less to do with *what* you do together than with whether you demonstrate a caring, others-centered attitude that reflects itself in your interaction. Gracious sophistication that keeps conversation moving along can be no more genuine than a salesman's smile when a well-heeled customer enters his store. Charm, verbal facility, cultural knowledge, and a quick wit have their place – but without a real interest in others as people God loves, they all add up to nothing.

The Bible provides no scripts for receiving guests, but it does tell us how a Christlike spirit will affect our speech. Here are a few principles from Proverbs:

Be slow to speak. "Reckless words pierce like a sword, but the tongue of the wise brings healing" (12:18). "He who guards his lips guards his life, but he who speaks rashly will come to ruin" (13:3). Listen to what people are really saying before you jump in with advice or criticism. When people are sharing a concern with you, they don't necessarily expect you to have an answer. Often they simply want to know that you're listening to them and trying to understand how they feel.

Be sensitive in your speech. "The mouth of the righteous is a fountain of life, but violence overwhelms the mouth of the wicked" (10:11). Ask yourself: "What words will be most effective in touching the person?" "What does the situation demand of me to help this person grow in Christ?"

Be gentle in your speech. "A gentle answer turns away wrath, but a harsh word stirs up anger" (15:1). "The tongue that brings healing is a tree of life, but a deceitful tongue crushes the spirit" (15:4).

Guests will feel received and welcomed in our homes when we sympathize with them in a compassionate, sensitive spirit. Rejoice with those who rejoice; mourn with those who mourn. Try not to tell others, "You shouldn't feel that way."

We should learn to open ourselves up with others so they are able to know us in a more personal way without burdening them with graphic details of all our past errors. Relating a personal experience that may offer help is often better received than impersonal advice. If we say, "Well, when this happened to me, I . . ." or "I think the Lord has always wanted me to behave in this way," our response will be more welcome than if we phrased it, "I think you should do this."

Telling about our feelings and personal experiences, especially when they demonstrate a way in which the Lord has worked in our lives, can be a powerful way to encourage others.

A short personal testimony can be a very helpful encouragement to others. First Corinthians 14:3 says, "The one who speaks God's message speaks to men and gives them help, encouragement and comfort." This does not mean that we need to repeat our entire life history each time we have a guest. However, we should always be prepared to give an account or "testify" of the way in which the Lord is working in our lives. "I learned the most exciting thing when I was reading the book of James this morning," is an example of an opening remark. "I really felt it was a blessing from the Lord when" or "A comment my son made yesterday really got my attention when he said," are also examples of beginnings to short accounts.

Think ahead about these testimonies while you are preparing for guests, or periodically while you are out driving or home standing at the kitchen sink. Reflect on one of the recent ways God has answered a prayer or made Himself known to you in a specific way. You may find that this exercise encourages *you* as much as your guest!

Pay careful attention to the words you say in conversation. "The tongue has the power of life and death" (Proverbs 18:21). Critical, condemning, judgmental, fault-finding words are *death words*. "An anxious heart weighs a man down, but a kind word cheers him up" (Proverbs 12:25). Kind words, forgiving, helpful, benevolent words are *life words*.

It may take extreme effort at first, but the more we strive to speak only living words and not killing words, the easier it becomes. We can only do this as our thoughts are held on living words, not death words. How I wish I could firmly imprint Philippians 4:8 on my heart and mind: "Whatever is true, whatever is noble, whatever is right, whatever is pure, whatever is lovely, whatever is admirable – if anything is excellent or praiseworthy – think about such things." This verse seems to sum up the ministry of encouraging others.

John wrote in 1 John 3:18, "Dear children, let us not love with words or tongue but with actions and in truth." When we offer hospitality to others, we are backing up our words with action.

IT HELPS TO PLAN AHEAD

It always helps to have a game plan. While I'm cleaning off the kitchen counter or setting the table, I try to think of a few questions I want to ask our guests to get to know them better. Here are a few ideas:

- ◆ How did you and your husband meet?
- ◆ Which person in your life was the most influential in leading you to the Lord?
- ◆ What is your favorite book of the Bible?
- ◆ How did you decide to live in our area?

These are just a few suggestions to get you thinking of questions you can ask your guests that can't be answered simply yes or no and should stimulate a conversation with some substance.

When I will be spending time with a close friend, I try to remember something that I know has been of concern to her that I can show I care about. "How is your mother?" "Is your relationship improving with your son?" "Are you feeling more comfortable in our community?" It is best not to ask these more personal questions right away, but do plan to get beyond surface relationships and share your concern on an intimate level.

Part of a game plan can be identifying a specific purpose for your hospitality in an upcoming visit. With one individual, your purpose may simply be to deepen your fellowship. With another, it may be to spur her on to do good works, to help her find her spiritual gifts and begin putting them to work. Or you may plan to show others by example how your faith works itself out in your life.

Remembering the difference between *goals* and *desires* can be really crucial in this area of purpose. For example, our goal may be to show our concern for a friend by the things we say and by our actions. Our desire may be that she share her feelings with us and feel encouraged. We should not be disappointed if she refuses to tell us how she feels. We can work to accomplish our goal of showing our concern and pray for our desire that she will respond. Our ability to encourage is enhanced if, while planning, we remember to keep our goals separate from our desires.

But not everything revolves around what we do or don't say. Letting others watch us in our own homes can be a ministry in itself. It is important that Christian families, especially those with children, invite less experienced couples to their homes to watch them and see effective Christian families in action. Isn't this what true discipleship really is? The same is true for every walk in the Christian life. Christian singles can demonstrate to others that you can have just as much "fun" living according to God's plan. Widows and widowers can remind each other that God is still with us when our spouse has gone. Mothers experiencing an empty nest for the first time can help others cope with the changes.

When I was a young mother, I learned more about mothering by watching other Christian mothers interact with their youngsters than I did by receiving instructions or reading books. The same was true when I learned effective ways of teaching Sunday school and leading a meeting and becoming a mother of teenagers. Offering hospitality in our homes gives us a powerful vehicle for demonstrating the pattern of our Christian lives in action.

WHEN THE CROWD JUST WALKED THROUGH THE DOOR

When you are hosting an event for a number of individuals, a "mixer" is often the best way to start things off. Try these ideas for encouraging guests to cut through their self-conscious layers and relax and enjoy each others' company.

Icebreaker Questions
Sit in a circle or at a table so you all have eye contact with each other and answer the same question in turn. Examples:

- If you could put one item from your childhood into a time capsule to tell something about yourself, what would it be?
- What has been the most important experience in your life?
- Who has been the most important person in your life and why?
- If you could visit any country in the world, where would you go and what would you see?
- What is your favorite season?
- What is your idea of a perfect evening?
- If you had to compare yourself with any type of animal, which one do you think you are most like? Why?
- How did you and your spouse meet?
- What is the greatest blessing God has given you?
- What three items you possess tell the most about the kind of person you are?
- If you could change one thing about yourself, what would you change?
- If you could live at any time in history, what period would it be?
- What is your favorite song? Dessert? Musical group?
- If you had one wish to be granted by a magic genie, what would it be?
- If you could look like any other person, who would it be?

Melody Match

This works well at Christmas, but it can be used at any time of year. Write out the words to a verse or two of a few well-known songs or Christmas carols. Then cut the words to the song into slips of paper with a few words on each. Give each guest one slip of paper. The guests have to mingle and find the individuals who have the rest of their song. When everyone has gotten the correct song and think they have put themselves in the correct order, each group takes its turn as individuals sing their portion of the song.

Photograph Explanation

I have never laughed as hard as I did when I attended a baby shower for couples where each guest was given a sheet of baby photos and asked to write a caption for each expression.

This game could be handled in a variety of ways. You can cut pictures out of magazines of faces with unique expressions and glue or tape them to pieces of paper. Or, you can keep a few snapshots of family members and friends specifically for use in this game, or purchase a paperback book with photographs of a comedian and use these. Give each guest a photograph or two and ask them to share their photo caption. (This game could also work with animal photographs using a *Ranger Rick* or *National Wildlife* magazine.)

Memory Game

Give each guest a piece of paper and a pencil. Carry around a tray or a basket filled with items that fit your party theme. Let each guest look at the items for fifteen seconds, then remove them from the room and see how many items each guest can remember.

The Mixer

When your guests RSVP, ask them to tell you something about themselves that others may not know. Then make a list of these bits of information to copy and then distribute to guests upon their arrival. Explain to them that they must guess which item describes whom. After confirming each item with the person it describes, they must have that person sign off on their list. This mixer helps people learn at least one new thing about each other and encourages conversation.

Here are a few examples from our last "mixer":

- ◆ Has a birthday this month
- ◆ Plays guitar
- ◆ Is an artist "of sorts"
- ◆ Wears contact lenses
- ◆ Has more than three children
- ◆ Grew up on a farm
- ◆ Won a beauty contest in high school
- ◆ Speaks two languages
- ◆ Has gone skiing this winter
- ◆ Has read the Bible through every year the last five years
- ◆ Had their car stuck in the snow this winter
- ◆ Has lived in five different states

Phrase Recognition

This icebreaker really stimulates conversation at the dinner table. As guests arrive, hand them each a well-known phrase or the title of something, such as a television show (a different one for each guest). Tell them to mention this phrase casually while you are all eating. The first person to recognize the phrase gets a point. For example, if you were using television shows, someone assigned "As the World Turns" might say, "It's been interesting to see all the changes in governments as the world turns." Someone else may say, "I'm not really sure how old she is – 'thirty something,' I guess." This icebreaker encourages talking as well as listening.

Word Scramble
Make a list of words that fit your party theme and scramble the letters up. The first person to unscramble all (or the most) words wins.

Bible Verse Matching
Make a list of Bible verses and their references. Let each guest match each verse to its reference. A related idea is matching up statements from the Bible with the names of the people who said them or the book of the Bible in which they appeared. Another variation of this is to list a few biblical events and see who can put them in the correct chronological order. These games are educational as well as fun.

Initial Message
Think of a slogan that will fit your theme, such as "Have a Happy Thanksgiving." Next, type or write a sheet of questions—one for each letter of your phrase. The first letter of each answer will spell out your phrase. Here is an example:

H Thanksgiving is a *(Holiday)*
A Written about oneself *(Autobiography)*
V Empty *(Vacant)*
E Two prophets having books in the Bible named for them *(Ezra/Ezekiel)*

A Runners, tennis players, pole vaulters, gymnasts *(Athletes)*

H The wicked king who sought to kill Jesus *(Herod)*
A A form of math *(Algebra)*
P A kind of pie we eat today *(Pumpkin)*

P We should do this without ceasing *(Pray/Praise)*

Y These are usually served at Thanksgiving *(Yams)*

T Gobble, gobble *(Turkey)*

H A girl's name and a kind of nut *(Hazel)*

A Another kind of pie from fruit *(Apple/Apricot)*

N Another word for a country *(Nation)*

K Used by a pianist or typist *(Keyboard)*

S Inside the turkey *(Stuffing)*

G The first book in the Bible *(Genesis)*

I Frozen water *(Ice)*

V An assortment *(Variety)*

I Delicious atop cakes or cookies *(Icing)*

N A place where plants grow *(Nursery)*

G The One to whom we should always give thanks *(God)*

Fairy Tale Headlines

How good is your memory? See if you and your guests can remember these fairy tales.

1. Cat with unusual footwear: *Puss-in-Boots*
2. Two children leave trail of pebbles (or bread crumbs): *Hansel & Gretel*
3. King's son climbs ladder made of girl's golden hair: *Rapunzel*
4. Princess loses golden ball: *Frog Prince*
5. This cookie ran away: *Gingerbread Boy*
6. Miller's daughter needs help spinning straw into gold: *Rumpelstiltskin*
7. Even his siblings were nasty to this web-footed character: *The Ugly Duckling*
8. She slept on a vegetable: *The Princess and the Pea*
9. He was the smallest boy in town: *Tom Thumb*

10. No one could put him together again: *Humpty Dumpty*
11. No one would help her bake the bread: *Little Red Hen*
12. Little girl who visits grandmother: *Little Red Riding Hood*
13. He thought the sky was falling: *Chicken Little*
14. Dark-haired girl finds several small friends: *Snow White*
15. Animals' house upset by small girl: *Goldilocks*
16. She witnessed a strange tea party: *Alice in Wonderland*
17. Her slipper was lost at curfew time: *Cinderella*
18. Boy sells family cow: *Jack and the Beanstalk*
19. Girl slept in a walnut shell: *Thumbelina*
20. Wooden puppet came to life: *Pinocchio*
21. A prince's kiss awakens this princess: *Sleeping Beauty*
22. Three children have an adventure in Neverland: *Peter Pan*
23. He stole from the rich: *Robin Hood*
24. The soldier had this amazing recipe: *Stone Soup*
25. This woman measured "practically perfect" (she also had a spoonful of sugar): *Mary Poppins*

Palindromes
Palindromes are words that are spelled the same way frontwards and backwards. "Sees" is an example. Here are a few others:

1. A notable achievement: *deed*
2. A flat, horizontal surface: *level*
3. More blood-colored: *redder*
4. Half a day past midnight: *noon*
5. Males and females: *sexes*

6. Made wet with dew: *dewed*
7. Samuel's mother: *Hannah*
8. Sound a chick makes: *peep*
9. Joshua's father: *Nun*
10. Part of the body: *eye*
11. Female sheep: *ewe*
12. To blow a horn in rapid blasts: *toot*
13. Musical compositions for a single voice: *solos*
14. A belief: *tenet*
15. A fool: *boob*
16. The monarchs of Iran: *shahs*
17. To allude to: *refer*
18. Soft drink: *pop*
19. A title of courtesy: *Madam*
20. What parents are called: *Mom, Dad*
21. Mechanical part that causes turning: *rotor*

Rhyming Answers
Here are a few descriptions of two words that rhyme, such as "mad dad" to describe an angry parent. Try your luck.

1. An obese rodent: *fat rat*
2. You should follow this in a place of learning: *school rule*
3. Child's playthings: *boy's toys*
4. Slender fruit ring: *thin skin*
5. A crazy young man: *mad lad*
6. A sugary delight or pleasure: *sweet treat*
7. A rodent in the home: *house mouse*
8. Liberty for a spelling contest: *bell spell*
9. Scarlet toboggan: *red sled*
10. A policeman – a store: *cop shop*
11. A term of endearment – a bird: *love dove*

12. This glass container is not near: *far jar*
13. An attractive, simple, short song: *pretty ditty*
14. A gloomy friend: *glum chum*
15. To occupy oneself in amusement for twenty-four hours: *play day*
16. Mislaid price tag: *lost cost*
17. A snobbish job: *snooty duty*
18. A burrowing animal—an opening: *mole hole*
19. To clip an arm or leg: *trim limb*
20. A bloodcurdling tale: *gory story*

Presidential Games

An encyclopedia or history book can give you multitudes of information for this novel icebreaker. For example, find a list of all the presidents of the United States. Then list another piece of information about each of them, such as either the state of their birth, their wife's name, their middle name, or a famous quotation from them. Your guests can try to match the items in these two lists. This game can also be used for states and their capitols and other bits of information.

Famous Quotations

Make a list of famous quotations or song titles and change one of the words. Have your guests try to correct your "mistakes." Here are examples from familiar sayings:

1. The more you save, the more you *want*. *(earn)*
2. Putting the cart before the *mule*. *(horse)*
3. All work and no play makes *Jerry* a dull boy. *(Jack)*
4. A *boy* and his money are soon parted. *(fool)*
5. The *consumer* is always right. *(customer)*
6. You learn something new every *morning*. *(day)*
7. You can't judge a book by its *title*. *(cover)*

8. You can't *bake* your cake and eat it too. *(have)*
9. You can't teach an old *cow* new tricks. *(dog)*
10. The *first* bird catches the worm. *(early)*
11. A rolling stone gathers no *mud*. *(moss)*
12. Blood is thicker than *wine*. *(water)*
13. An apple a day keeps the *teacher* away. *(doctor)*
14. A *pitcher* is worth a thousand words. *(picture)*
15. It's no use *laughing* over spilled milk. *(crying)*

Name That Wife

A fitting name for an oysterman's wife might be Pearl. Here are a few occupations. Match them with the name that would fit.

1. Lawyer	a. Hazel
2. Capitalist	b. Penny
3. Civil engineer	c. Winnie
4. Bird watcher	d. Wyn
5. Athlete	e. Olive
6. Sexton	f. Eileen
7. Nutcracker	g. Sandy
8. Chef	h. Kitty
9. Singer	i. Candie
10. Banker	j. Bridget
11. Fruit picker	k. Carol
12. Horseman	l. Gail
13. Confectioner	m. Sue
14. Acrobat	n. Iris
15. Apiarist	o. Bea
16. Toymaker	p. Ione
17. Ophthalmologist	q. Dolly
18. Veterinarian	r. Belle
19. Meteorologist	s. Robin
20. Beachcomber	t. Cherry

Answers: 1. m   2. p   3. j   4. s   5. d   6. r   7. a   8. e
9. k   10. b   11. t   12. c   13. i   14. f   15. o   16. q
17. n   18. h   19. 1   20. g

These are just a few ideas for ice breakers. Books are also available with game ideas. Be creative and think of your own ideas. Keep your goal in mind: Help people relax and get to know each other better.

NOTES
1. Lawrence J. Crabb, Jr., and Dan B. Allender, *Encouragement: The Key to Caring* (Grand Rapids: Zondervan, Pyranee Books, 1984), pages 114-115.
2. Adapted from Crabb and Allender, pages 114-116.

Chapter 6

❖

ENCOURAGEMENT BEGINS AT HOME

O ne of my favorite passages is 1 Corinthians 13:1-3 —"If I speak in the languages of men and of angels, but have not love, I am only a resounding gong or a clanging cymbal. If I have the gift of prophecy and can fathom all mysteries and all knowledge, and if I have a faith that can move mountains, but have not love, I am nothing. If I give all I possess to the poor and surrender my body to the flames, but have not love, I am nothing." I like to paraphrase this passage to remind myself: If I offer hospitality that is impressive but not loving, it is worth nothing. If I offer hospitality to everyone in the world but forget to offer it to my own family, I have wasted my time.

Paul reminds us of this priority on the family in 1 Timothy 5:8—"If anyone does not provide for his relatives, and especially for his immediate family, he has denied the faith and is worse than an unbeliever."

THE GIFT OF OUTSIDE INFLUENCE

Even if you're without an extended family of your own, please don't skip over this chapter. Single people and couples without children of their own can reach out to nieces and nephews and children in their neighborhoods and their church. Grandparents can minister to their own grandchildren and "adopted" grandchildren. My most valuable assistant when I was preparing for children's parties was a very creative single friend. Her interest in my children's lives was irreplaceable.

A friend told me years ago when her sixteen-year-old daughter was going through a rough time, "Rachael, I have always prayed for the positive influence of a godly older woman in my daughter's life. Thank you for being that person." I thoroughly enjoyed being a part of her daughter's life and was thrilled that I had influenced her to draw closer to the Lord. My friend reminded me, "Don't forget to pray for someone like that to come into your boys' lives."

I remembered her advice and prayed for a godly man to appear in our lives and be a positive influence for Keplen and Kenton. I knew that Larry and I couldn't possibly meet every one of our boys' needs. That's what the extended Body of Christ is for.

A few years later, a Bible teacher came from California to our church in Florida to give a discipleship class. He challenged all the college students to "adopt" a family. Soon after, a young man who was a college student and one of six children in his family came to Larry and volunteered to watch our two sons during the summer. When Larry shared this news with me, I thought it sounded too good to be true. I decided I wasn't going to hold my breath, though I knew Ray had been sincere in his offer.

I was surprised when Ray called me one day to announce that he and his brother, Dean, had tickets to the Fort Lauderdale Strikers soccer game and they wanted to take Keplen and Kenton with them. That evening was the beginning of a wonderful relationship between my sons and Ray.

Through the summer, twice a week, Ray and Dean would arrive at our door to take the boys someplace special. They always had a great time. When the boys were small, Larry used a chalkboard to illustrate their devotional talks. He left the illustrations when he was finished. When Ray and Dean would return with Kep and Ken, my sons would explain the devotion to them. I think our young sons impacted Ray and Dean as much as they were influenced.

When we moved, Ray continued to keep in touch with the boys. He wrote to them all the following summer and kept in touch. Kep still has the marvelous letter of encouragement Ray wrote to him when he graduated from high school.

Ray is now a pastor in Florida, and Dean pastors a church in North Carolina. I am thankful for the personal touch they gave our sons in answer to my prayers. I believe the Lord honored their commitment to encourage our sons by giving them a special blessing and deepening their spiritual growth through the process.

MAKING FAMILY MEMBERS FEEL SPECIAL

I'll never forget the evening I discovered how important it was to my young children that we have special evenings just for them. We had invited a dear old friend of the family over for dinner. The kids helped me set a beautiful table using our best dishes and a cloth table covering. The meal I had prepared was no different than our usual evening fare, but I had made an extra effort to serve it with a flair.

Our guest forgot to come! When I was afraid the roast

would be totally ruined and we were all starving, I called her house and found out she had gone out of town for the day. I rounded up our family, and we ate our supper at the dining room table with cloth napkins and candles.

The children were more excited about the meal than if we had shared it with company. I felt so guilty when one of them said, "Mom, you never do this for just us!"

"You are more important to me than anyone else in the world," I assured them. We had a wonderful evening, right down to the fresh whipped cream on the frozen chocolate pie.

I learned an important lesson that evening. When my family sees me making a special effort to encourage others, I must be doubly sure I make the effort to encourage them. Occasionally that means having a special evening just for our family.

Often the things that make the biggest difference take only a little effort. I use special decorations for all the holidays and pretty napkins or a distinctive centerpiece for special days. I would go out of my way even though I was never really sure if my sons or husband ever noticed.

I finally received a word of encouragement years later when Ken came home from college one day with a friend. When the two young men came in the front door, I overheard Ken tell his friend, "See, Mike, I told you my mom would have the house decorated for Saint Patrick's Day. She always knows how to make us feel special."

When Kep was twenty-one, he told Larry, "When I think of Mom, I think of home and all the neat things she did for us that I didn't really appreciate until I left home." What an honor to be able to make our own families feel special.

I have often wondered why young people tend to congregate at some homes and seem to avoid others. As

I have observed my sons and their friends over the years, I have discovered that the wealth of the home, the material embellishments, the neighborhood, and whether there's food in the refrigerator all have little to do with making a home the place to be. All people, whether young or old, want to be in a place where they feel comfortable and accepted, and are encouraged.

We can all create an atmosphere of comfort for our families and their friends. This doesn't mean we don't have house rules; reasonable limits are an important part of creating a comfortable environment. It does mean freedom from a critical spirit. Instead, a spirit of encouragement should fill our home. Our attitude should be, "I love you because God loves you. He cared enough for you to die on the cross for your sins, and you are special to Him. I respect you for who you are and for what God created you to be, and I can see in you the person you can become with God's help." That type of atmosphere is hard for anyone to resist. And it must start within our own family before it will be evident to anyone else. Consider the following suggestions for ways to make your family feel special.

IDEAS FOR CREATIVE FAMILY TIMES

Indoor Picnic
Some of our best times have been impromptu family parties. One afternoon in the dead of winter, we spread a blanket on the family room floor, blew up a few beach toys, and packed a picnic basket with peanut butter and jelly sandwiches, chips, and apples. (Once I made it even easier by picking up fried chicken and the trimmings from a fast food restaurant.) I pulled some house plants over to the edge of the blanket and spread a few plastic

ants across to add a touch of realism. We sat on the blanket to eat our meal, read a few books, and imagined how our toes felt in the sand.

You can even wear your sunglasses, but don't forget to enjoy the lovely weather!

Camp-In

Another simple way to throw a party for your family is to have an indoor camp-out. Put the sleeping bags on the floor, light a candle or use flashlights, and eat hot dogs. Tell stories and sing camp songs. Have a special testimony sharing time. Pretending to camp out is especially exciting for young children who may not be quite ready to brave the real outdoors, complete with mosquitos and scary noises. Having a camp-out also provides a unique opportunity to tell stories about your childhood and dreams of the future. Add authenticity to "camp-ins" by roasting hot dogs and marshmallows in the fireplace on cold winter evenings. You can always melt marshmallows in the microwave or over burners as a last resort. Children who have spent time at church camp often have songs and stories to share.

Movie Night

Rent a special movie or two, turn the lights down low, pop popcorn, buy licorice, and spend a night at the movies. If you have an answering machine, turn it on so you won't be interrupted for the duration of the movie—or just unplug the phone. At the end, ask your children to describe their favorite part of the movie. What was the funniest? What did they think was the scariest? Which character would they most like to be?

Even when we go to a real movie theater, we always share these same questions on the way home. It helps keep the spirit of the evening alive all the way home and creates a good opportunity for discussion. If the movie was disappointing, discuss your displeasure with the plot or a character's actions. Why don't we want to act like that? How could faith in God have helped? What can we learn from this?

Talent Shows

Children of all ages enjoy displaying their talents. Recite Bible verses or poems, play a tune on the piano, or sing a song. Read from a favorite book. My children loved to turn the footstool on its side and use it as a stage for puppet shows. Watching young people write their own dramas gives you insight into their character and their ideas of life.

Even teenagers can be coaxed into demonstrating their latest soccer or skateboard skills, practicing an impromptu barbershop quartet, or performing an improvisational skit.

Dawn is a creative preschool teacher. When young friends visit her, she reads them a few of her favorite poems and nursery rhymes. She reads through a story with the youngsters and then lets them choose a character from that story. After the children practice, she reads the story for the parents while the children act out their parts. Even very young children enjoy acting out *The Three Kittens Who Lost Their Mittens, Peter Cottontail,* or *The Three Little Pigs.* Youngsters also enjoy miming songs that are playing on the record player or radio.

My Sunday school class of third and fourth graders once practiced and performed a play for the rest of the Sunday school classes. We were studying the book of Esther, so I wrote a play and made as many parts as possible to accommodate each child in the class. We used bunny puppets for Esther and Mordecai and bears for the eunuchs. The oldest, shabbiest puppet we could find became the evil Haman, and Miss Piggy was the arrogant Queen Vashti. We had special practices on two Saturdays and ordered pizza at the end of our last practice. The young people enjoyed the practices as much as performing the play, and it really helped them remember the book of Esther and the principles it taught.

Giving a Special Word
A favorite Crabb birthday tradition is "giving a word." We give the birthday person a unique word for the day that describes one of their special attributes or talents. It may be a word from a favorite Bible verse. One year, Larry gave me the word *bouncebackedness*. I always cherish the special birthday words my husband and sons give me.

One Thanksgiving we visited my parents and celebrated my sister's birthday. Her son gave her the word *unselfish*; her daughter gave her *creative*. I told her she was *kind* and Larry gave her the word *committed*. Her husband simply said, "Mine."

You could choose a special word from Scripture with a corresponding quote: "courageous" with Joshua 1:7 — "Be strong and very courageous. Be careful to obey all the law my servant Moses gave you; do not turn from it to the right or to the left, that you may be successful wherever you go."

A Special Book
Larry has always written letters to our boys on their birthdays. They each have a leather three-ring notebook imprinted with their name and the words, "Controlled by Truth." These words are a reminder to Kep and Ken

of the key passages about Scripture in Psalm 119:160 and 2 Timothy 3:14-17.

Larry covers all sorts of subjects in these letters: advice on being a man, growing in the Lord, how he feels about them. The subjects may be varied, but the main thrust of each is the same: to give encouragement.

On their birthday, Larry always takes our sons out for lunch or dinner for a special father/son discussion. Each year he asks them the same questions: What do you like best about yourself? What do you like least? What do you like best and least about me, your mother, your brother? Where do you find beauty? What do you want to do when you grow up? How do you feel spiritually? Where do you find your greatest joy?

Soon after their birthday dinner, Larry writes down the answers to these questions and his thoughts about their evening together. When each of our sons celebrated his twenty-first birthday, Larry typed up all the questions and answers of the past years and presented them to be added to their birthday book. It was a special view of their first twenty-one years.

Larry writes to me on our anniversary. In my book entitled "Companion by Covenant, Genesis 2:24," I keep the cards and letters Larry has given to me over the years. What an encouragement this book has been to me!

There are so many ways to celebrate birthdays. My friend Gloria was so excited about bearing three healthy children after losing two that she determined to make her children's birthdays extra-special celebrations. One year she brought pizza to school at lunchtime for her son's entire class to celebrate that the Lord had spared both mother and son on the day of his birth in their very close brush with death. What a testimony that was for the entire school!

Gloria also takes her birthday child out for a special lunch or dinner at the restaurant of his or her choice. She ate a lot of fast food in the early years!

I have a huge plastic banner that I tape across the front of the house on birthdays to announce it to the entire neighborhood. I tape my son's photograph to a poster that says, "Kiss the birthday person." The most important rule of the day is to make the birthday person the center of attention.

BIRTHDAY PARTIES

As children get older, activity parties are a great choice. Parties at a skating rink, pool, or gymnasium are fun, and there's no huge mess to clean up at the end. Local restaurants often have birthday specials where youngsters can make their own pizza, see how doughnuts are made, or take a tour of the restaurant.

Younger children usually enjoy having a party at their own home. Here are a few ideas:

Hot Air Balloon Party

For my son's fifth birthday party, I decorated cupcakes to look like hot air balloons by placing three straws in each cupcake and taping a balloon to the top. I found a balloon centerpiece and decorated the house with balloons. I froze water in balloons and floated them in the punch bowl to keep the punch cold.

The entertainment was simple. The children had a relay race with balloons tucked between their knees. Then we tied balloons to their ankles with curling ribbon, and they tried to break other balloons without popping their own. The children ate hotdogs, chips, ice cream, and their balloon cupcakes as the presents were opened.

It's always nice to give every child at the party a little something to take home. Some inexpensive ideas include bubble-blowing bottles, coloring books and crayons, small airplanes, plastic dinosaurs, jacks, balloons, or Bible story books.

Pink Fairyland

The most beautifully decorated house I've ever seen was at the thirteenth birthday party for my friend's daughter. Ann hung pink and white netting all through the house to turn their home into a fairyland. She blew up silver, white, and pink balloons and decorated with flowers. As guests arrived, she handed out strands of inexpensive "pearls" (bought by the dozen from a catalog) and a wand with a silver, glittery star on the end of it. The girls all felt like princesses through the entire evening.

A decorated cake, pink punch, and crustless sandwiches cut into shapes served on pink paper plates seemed like a feast to the princesses.

A Hawaiian Luau

Ginger's birthday party began at her house and ended up at the local pool. When her guests arrived, they were given a plastic lei and a tissue flower was pinned in their hair. As the honored birthday girl, Ginger wore a dimestore tiara. All the girls were encouraged to "dress Hawaiian" and bring their swimsuits.

Music from the islands was played on the stereo, and the centerpiece was a cut pineapple filled with fresh fruit. Swimming in the pool gave them plenty to do.

A Trip to Outer Space

Boys especially love outer space. You can usually find some current character or movie to help decorate this theme party. Presents wrapped in aluminum foil with silver and blue ribbons can serve as centerpieces. Give the guests small boxes, paper towel rolls, glue, tape, and aluminum foil and let them create their own spaceships. A scavenger hunt can plant clues to find treasure in a galaxy far, far away.

Check novelty stores or catalogs for headbands with springs and antennae or ray guns. Games can include making paper airplanes (whose flew the farthest?) and guessing the names of the planets.

Sports Parties Can Be a Ball

A single layer, round cake can be frosted with brown frosting and black string licorice for the "stitching" to turn it into a baseball glove. Red licorice whips turn white cupcakes into baseballs.

Relay races, baseball throws, batting balloons are all fun games for active youngsters. Hand out baseball cards for take-home gifts.

HOLIDAY CELEBRATIONS

Our family loves to celebrate Easter with egg hunts. When young children are here, we hide plastic eggs filled with goodies all over the yard. We used to hide the boys' Easter baskets and give them clues to go from one place to another. Sometimes the clues would rhyme; other times the clues were about them; one Easter the clues were about biblical stories and the baskets were hidden outside. The clue, "look where Zacchaeus went to see Jesus" meant the next clue was stuck in a tree. "Look at the place like the one where Jesus cooked breakfast for the disciples" meant the clue was hidden in the campfire pit.

Coloring Easter eggs and writing names on them

with wax crayons has become a family tradition.

When our sons were young, Larry would give them clues to find their money from the "tooth fairy." Kep's clues one year were:

#1 — Go to where you listen to "Jailhouse Rock."
#2 — An apple a day keeps the doctor away. Eat fruit from the fruit bowl.
#3 — Your brother plays tennis. Look for his trophy.

The clues were all simple, but the looking was such fun!

Summer opens up many opportunities for special family outings: a trip to the beach or the zoo, watching fireworks on the fourth of July, having picnics, holding family reunions. My sister hollows out a huge watermelon when we have picnics and fills it with soda pop. Sometimes she puts the lid back on the watermelon with holes for straws and lets everyone join in.

Thanksgiving is an ideal opportunity to praise the Lord and celebrate family traditions. Even when we have company at our home, we always take time before we eat to share with each other the things we're thankful for.

Sometimes the best way to encourage someone out of town is to go visit them. One year we traveled across the state to visit friends. It was their first Thanksgiving after their grandfather had died. He had always cooked the turkey, and we knew this year would be an especially difficult time for them. We brought games and food and helped them begin some new traditions that year.

One year, when the kids were very young, we were not having company, and I was too exhausted to cook a huge meal. We knew a woman who lived in a nursing home who had no plans for the day. She no longer recognized anyone in her family, and it had become too painful to them to visit her. We invited Maizie to go out for dinner with us. We enjoyed each other's company, and I had no dirty dishes to wash!

Christmas is another great season for family traditions. We always insisted that the boys match the total amount of money they spent on gifts for family members to buy a special gift for someone outside the family. One year we helped them buy a used refrigerator for an acquaintance who had fourteen children and didn't have a refrigerator. We emphasized that Christmas is a time for giving because Christ gave so much for us.

We have friends who go shopping to purchase necessary items and gifts to fill a shoe box for Friends of the Americas.[1] They include a photograph and a letter to their "friend" in South America. When their son Rick was packing his box intended for a boy his age, he put in the underwear and socks, toothbrush, silverware, safety pins, and Band-Aids without comment. When he added the paper and crayons, he exclaimed to his mother, "You mean these children don't even have their own crayons? You mean if they want to draw, they have to use their finger in the sand?" To Rick, total poverty meant not having crayons. Packing a shoe box full of gifts for another child helped him understand the meaning of Christmas in an immediate way.

An advent wreath, special devotions, a birthday cake for Jesus, a nativity scene set out on a small table where young hands can reach the baby Jesus and move the shepherds and camels around, all give special meaning to a very special holiday.

As important as it is to offer hospitality to others and make guests feel special, there are times when we need to step back, be alone with our families, and rest.

Last year, Larry and I were under a great deal

of pressure from hectic schedules. Larry was juggling speaking engagements, book deadlines, and counseling demands. I was consulting with several churches on their women's ministries, speaking to groups, and running our household. It seemed we were passing each other in the night.

At the time, Kent and Karla were living with us. They sensed our near exhaustion. Karla was bedridden with a difficult pregnancy, but that didn't keep her from ministering to us. From her bed, she made a huge banner that Kent hung in front of our house. The banner read, "Home Is a Haven Week." For several days, our home was our haven. Karla intercepted unnecessary phone calls and Kent ran interference so Larry and I could rest.

Home can truly become a haven when it is built on the cornerstone of Jesus Christ and supported by the loving commitment of family members to encourage each other day by day.

NOTE
1. Friends of the Americas is a nonprofit public charity that organizes people-to-people programs and operates medical clinics, schools, and other facilities in Latin America. Gifts are hand delivered to needy children in fifteen countries. Friends of the Americas is located at 912 North Foster Drive, Baton Rouge, LA 70806.

Chapter 7

HOSPITALITY THAT TRAVELS

I was exhausted. I had been working long hours for weeks. I longed for a week of uninterrupted sleep — or even just a leisurely hour chatting with a good friend over a cup of tea.

One afternoon, in the midst of activity, I received a small package in the mail. It came with the instructions, "Take this box into a secluded room — by yourself — and open when you have a few moments of privacy."

Needless to say, my curiosity got the best of me, and I soon managed to find a few moments to hide in my bedroom and open the box. A friend, who lived hundreds of miles away, had sensed my near exhaustion during a recent telephone conversation and sent me this care package full of tiny, inexpensive, individually wrapped gifts.

Each gift bore a message. I unwrapped a delicate fan, some tiny pewter animals, a cameo necklace, a small devotional book. My favorite gift was an elaborate, lacy handkerchief that was beautiful but very wrinkled. The note on this gift said, "Sorry about the wrinkles, but I gave up ironing for Lent in 1979." One small package contained a single bath cube with the instructions, "Use this for one leisurely, hot bath to melt away your cares

The most important message I found in the box was the one that said my friend was praying for me. She knew I was tired and in need of renewal. Her care package did more for my spirits than a week's worth of sleep. None of the items in the parcel was expensive; not all of them were even new. The thought behind them was the lovely hospitality that crossed the miles. I felt as if we had shared a comforting hour of companionship over a pot of tea.

KEEP THOSE CARDS AND LETTERS COMING

Ramona, a woman in our Bible study, seldom voices her concerns or ideas with our group. She never volunteers to lead the lesson, though we all take turns leading the group. She is quiet by nature.

A few weeks ago, Ramona reluctantly volunteered to try to lead our next lesson. We all encouraged her. I knew she was nervous about preparing for our study in Hebrews, so I sent her a note to tell her we were all praying for her and to relax and enjoy studying. I assured her that with the Lord's help she would do a wonderful job. I later received the following note from her in the mail:

> Thanks so much for the card. I really appreciate
> it. And more importantly, *thanks for your prayers!!*
> I worked hard at preparing the lesson, and when
> I first started giving it, I was nervous, but after
> a little while, when we got into it, it was fun!
> Deb and Diana said they had been praying for
> me too.

Ramona went on in her note to give me encouragement, too. She promised to remember me in her prayers.

Ramona and I have different personalities. She is older than I and more reserved. We don't communicate as well in person as we do through written words. I can have more of a ministry to Ramona by sending her notes and praying for her than by inviting her to our home for a meal.

The important thing is to "spur one another on to good works." If we can spend five minutes and a postage stamp to send an encouraging note to another person to make it possible for her to do something new for the Lord—whether preparing a Bible study lesson, teaching a Sunday school class, or growing in Christian maturity—what an investment that little expenditure has been!

When I was in college, every Monday I sent a postcard to each of the two single women who had raised my mother. I couldn't even afford the pretty cards with photographs, but I'm sure they appreciated getting a note from me each week.

Cards, notes, and letters can be powerful ways to send encouragement. Send congratulations, happy birthday, get well. Send someone a card for no special reason. I remember a miserable day when I received a card with a cute porcupine on the front and a silly message. I had a good laugh, which was exactly what I needed to make my way through the day.

When my sister-in-law Linda lived in Saint Louis, the members of their church were looking forward to the arrival of a new pastor who was coming in six months. Linda bought sixty different picture postcards of Saint Louis, stamped them, and distributed them to families in the church who promised to send them to the new pastor. So many church families got involved in mailing greetings to the pastor and his family that Linda purchased additional postcards. Imagine how welcome the new pastor and his family felt as they prepared to come minister at this new church.

We often overlook a golden opportunity to encourage others when they have done something well. When an associate has worked hard on a project, made posters for your women's group, led an exciting Bible study, gotten good grades on a report card, obtained a master's degree—send an encouraging note. When someone has fixed something broken at church, written a good letter to the editor, volunteered at the local hospital or nursing home, represented your community well as a state representative—send an encouraging note.

I enjoy sewing and have made a number of bears over the years. When Kep's college roommate announced his engagement, Kep "borrowed" his pillowcase. I turned his bachelor pillowcase into a bear and gave it to his fiancee as a shower gift. I have enjoyed making bears for friends that match a specific room or remind them of a special person or event.

Traveling hospitality does not have to be wrapped up in silver ribbons and expensive wrapping paper. If friends are some distance away, mail them flower bulbs, which are easily planted and bloom year after year.

Jane keeps a birthday and anniversary notebook with pockets to help her remember special events through the year. "One year my resolution was to send my friends and everyone in my family birthday cards," she told me. "I kept my resolution, but the following year, I expanded it. My new resolve was to remember everyone's birthday—on time!" Jane keeps a few boxes of cards on hand and buys any additional cards for the following month. At the beginning of each month, she signs the cards for that month and marks the birthdate on the corner of the envelope where she will put the stamp so she will remember to mail them in plenty of time. Jane keeps her cards with her mail and adds the stamp on the day she takes the card to the post office.

Jane commented, "It's amazing to me how much closer I've become to one of my cousins, just because I have remembered her birthday for the past few years. I've really noticed a change in her attitude, just because she knows there are people who care for her. I think she is beginning to realize that if I can care for her and I'm just a person, how much more God must care for her."

CARE PACKAGES FOR ANY OCCASION

Traveling hospitality can take a variety of forms. Here are a few ideas for care packages:

Someone in Jail
- stamps
- writing paper or stationery
- birthday or holiday cards that they can send to others
- photographs
- good reading material

Someone in a Nursing Home
- knee-high pantyhose
- lotions/powder
- a pretty wall hanging
- large-print reading material
- one silk flower
- colorful balloons
- soft, cuddly stuffed animal
- a pretty bed pillow
- a warm bed-jacket or sweater

- pajamas or nightgown
- warm slippers
- stamps, greeting cards
- Bring a child to share a hug and kiss and home-made drawing storybook to read to young visitors.
- Offer to take them on an outing or run an errand for them.

Someone in the Service or Away at College

- homemade cookies/candy
- toiletries: shampoo, toothpaste, etc.
- packages of hot chocolate, instant soup
- stamps, cards, notepaper
- little picture album with a few photographs already in it
- food, food, food

A Lonely Friend

- bubble bath
- pretty napkins
- herbal tea
- small craft item, such as a cross-stitch ornament
- devotional book
- special Bible verse written on a pretty notecard
- empty notebook to record thoughts and prayers
- box or package of cards to send to others (with stamps)
- pretty dish towels
- gift certificate for two to a restaurant
- small tins of jams or jellies or fancy cookies

A Young Person

- stickers
- balloons

- puzzles, games, books
- magnets

Dawn had a wonderful birthday gift for her godchild. Knowing how the girl loved "teaching school," Dawn found a large plastic shopping bag from a school supply store. She made a name tag, encased in plastic, trimmed with a bow, which read, "Miss Prater." She filled the bag with a red pencil (for grading papers), a stencil book, homemade flash cards, some plain paper, construction paper, a hole-puncher, and worksheets. Dawn had a wonderful way of encouraging "Miss Prater" to improve her teaching skills.

A New Mother
- a letter offering Bible verses and anecdotes from your early mothering years
- an IOU for babysitting
- cuddly toy
- lullaby tape
- subscription to or copy of *Christian Parenting* magazine
- one-year calendar
- short devotionals — with a note that she will have time to read long ones again someday!
- a list of your child's favorite toys at that age

When I was in the hospital to have my first son, a dear friend brought me a delicate necklace and perfumed body lotion. It was such a wonderful treat. I was exhausted and had no energy even to put on makeup, but my necklace made me feel pretty and the lotion made me feel soft and smell wonderful. I felt like a lovely lady, even though I was a physical wreck!

Someone Coping With Illness or Grief at Home
My friend Gloria was trapped at home with two sick daughters. Jillian was a bouncy first-grader and Melissa, a quickly maturing fifth-grader. I suspected that by the end of the week, Gloria must have been getting a bit weary in her role as mother and nursemaid to two very different daughters. I called to make sure they were still at home. A very tired voice answered the telephone. "No, we aren't going anywhere," was her reply.

I made a quick trip to a bookstore and a dime store. I spent only a few dollars and filled a sack with a coloring book, punch-out book, "How to Draw Monsters" activity book, colored markers, 100-piece puzzle, and several inexpensive card games. When I arrived at the temporary hospital, the love seat and couch had been transformed into forts—a sure sign that the patients were recovering. I asked the girls to promise to share any surprises that I might have in my sack. (Actually, the gifts were more for their Mom than for them.) Gloria admitted later that the sack full of surprises really helped them survive the weekend.

If I hadn't had a few dollars, I could have loaned them a few of our games, torn a few pages out of partially used coloring books, rounded up some extra stickers, and found leftover Sunday school papers. What's important is not whether you spend money, but that you share a bit of hospitality.

You can practice traveling hospitality by bringing someone lunch or just giving her a phone call to show you care. I could have stayed with the girls for an hour and sent their mother to the library to check out a good book and enjoy a few moments of quiet.

When Patsy's husband died, a caring friend gave her a stack of TV dinners all tied up with a bow. That was a very thoughtful gift for someone who would be cooking for one and missing her dinner partner. Frozen desserts or TV dinners tied up with ribbon accompanied by a package of pretty napkins would be a considerate gift for single friends, too.

Someone in the Hospital
- flowers or balloons
- reading material (perhaps even a television listing)
- Loan a cassette player with soothing music tapes, tapes of the latest church service; include a blank tape to record messages.
- Give a manicure or pedicure. You should not put colored nail polish on hospital patients (the nurses need to be able to check their fingernails), but you can put lotion on their hands and feet and buff and file their nails. Could our model here be Jesus washing His disciples' feet?
- Bring a good book and read aloud. A selection of poetry or short stories would be nice. Read something uplifting.
- Take dictation for a letter or message to someone.

When hospitalized after being pinned under a car, Chris was so concerned about all the stitches and swelling in his face that he asked for photographs of himself to be hung over his hospital bed so his nurses would know how he really looked. His mother taped his get-well cards all over the walls of his room just like wallpaper to cheer him. Special friends brought him ice cream and pizza and even arranged short visits from young friends who didn't qualify for traditional visiting regulations. An occasional helium balloon or chocolate chip cookie was delivered. The extra "traveling hospitality" helped Chris recover completely. Today, Chris is a compassionate college student who visits others in the hospital and offers encouragement with empathy and understanding.

When you want to help those at home who have a family member in the hospital, consider these suggestions. When you bring them food, put it in a disposable or nonreturnable container. Good choices of foods include stews, casseroles, soups, brownies, cheese and crackers, fresh fruit, and frozen dishes.

I'll never forget when Ann's husband was in the hospital and a well-meaning woman brought over gallons of soup. An army couldn't have consumed all that soup; it would spoil long before it could be eaten for twenty-five meals in a row. It's better to send smaller portions, or items that can be frozen and heated when most convenient for the family.

Instead of making a general offer to help, volunteer to perform a specific task. "Can I wash your dishes or vacuum your home?" "Could I walk the dog for you, or would you rather I take home your ironing?" "Could I mow your yard, or do you have a specific yard chore that needs to be done?"

A friend told me that when a death in the family required them to pack their bags in a hurry, the kindest help came from an elderly neighbor. He arrived at their home with an offer to polish all their shoes. "While you are packing," he said, "give me all your shoes and I'll polish them so you have shiny shoes for the funeral." That was true encouragement. He offered the talent that he could share.

When the families from our office were traveling from Indiana to Colorado, I sent a shoe box with each family. I put notes on the box with directions. "Open the package with this sticker when you see a bird on a cow's back." "Open this package when you cross the Illinois state line."

A rubber ball, jump rope, and bubbles were coded, "Open this package when you arrive at a rest stop to enjoy your picnic lunch." Sunglasses were wrapped with the directions, "Open this package when the sun comes up." Plastic combs were wrapped for "when you arrive at your motel." I would have loved to have been with them on their trip, but since I could not, I sent a little of myself along the way with them.

When we moved to the Midwest from Florida, I could not always find the time to send letters to my dear friends. I also longed to share a little of the beauty of our autumn, so I mailed them envelopes filled with colorful autumn leaves. An elderly friend managed to "outdo" my efforts. He mailed me an envelope filled with sand and sandburrs—a reminder of days in Florida.

In the course of our lives, I think the small acts of kindness we have received will long remain in our memories. The plant we received for a birthday, the cookies someone brought over when we came home from the hospital, the kind word contained in a card that cheered us just as we felt like giving up—all these have been vehicles for God's love to come to us through human lives.

As we make an effort to practice traveling hospitality, God will enlarge our ministry for Him. He will give us fresh opportunities and rewarding experiences.

Chapter 8

❖

RELAX!

When we were in England for three months while Larry was writing a book, there were a number of young men living in our building who were working on their Ph.D. or doing postgraduate work.

These men were extremely comfortable with books, but totally unaccustomed to practicing hospitality. Larry and I enjoyed inviting them to our flat for sweets, meals, and a Christmas tea. We all got to know each other in a much more personal way. I was surprised when several of them mentioned they had never been invited to anyone's flat before.

When we were preparing to return to the States, these men demonstrated how contagious practicing hospitality can be. One afternoon, they invited Larry and me to join them for a meal in the common room. I had no idea that they had planned the meal in our honor. Each of the eight men had taken responsibility for a part of the meal. One baked bread, another purchased a card, one wrote a poem, another prepared dessert. I was overwhelmed. Larry and I had demonstrated our concern for them by sharing with them, and they had learned how to encourage through hospitality.

Soon after we arrived in England, I volunteered for teatime. Each person in the building was to take a turn at preparing the tea every afternoon for one week. This usually amounted to boiling water and adding the tea. Those interested would drift into the common room throughout the afternoon to get a cup of tea.

I was determined to break the ice with our neighbors. The first day I prepared the tea and served cookies. The second day I served candies, followed by baskets of fruit the following day. On Thursday, I served cheese and crackers—and by now everyone was coming to tea. On my last day we had all the leftovers from the past four days and had a wonderful time becoming better acquainted. The comment I received that meant the most to me was, "You act as if you care about us."

Isn't that the highest purpose for practicing hospitality? If we demonstrate our concern for others, they are much more likely to listen to our words and want to become better acquainted with our Lord.

FOCUS ON OTHERS

Hospitality is *not* trying to impress someone with our decorating or culinary ability. True hospitality strives to encourage others, to bring them closer to the Lord, to get to know them better or to have fellowship with them. When practicing hospitality, you focus your thought and attention on others and make them feel comfortable. Then you feel less stress and more joy, and you can truly enjoy sharing yourself with others.

Christie came to my home for Bible study one evening deeply distressed. That afternoon, as she was leaving a store in a busy shopping center, she had watched a mother slap her infant child several times. "What should

I have done?" Christie asked us. "I was afraid if I said something to her she would be even more cruel to her baby after I left. I just didn't know what to do!"

Because I cared enough to invite Christie into my home, she was sharing her pain with me and asked for advice. But I had no idea what to say to her. I silently asked the Lord to give me words of wisdom. It is so difficult to know how to respond to the violence and cruelty in this world.

I was surprised when these words came out of my mouth: "Christie, what happened today was terrible, and I can see that you are extremely upset. I don't know why things like this happen, except that this is a sinful world and people are in need of accepting God's love. I can see that you have been affected by this experience, and the Bible promises that God can bring good out of every situation for those of us who love Him—including this one. Perhaps God will use this experience today to prepare you to have a ministry to do something to stop child abuse."

I wrote Christie's name in my prayer diary and continued to pray for her and the mother and the poor baby who had been mistreated.

Less than a year later, I attended a women's meeting with a program on child abuse. Here was Christie in charge of the program. She had joined our county's child abuse council. She had gotten statistics from our state and county and interviewed local nurses and pastors to gain insight and information. She set out pamphlets and showed us an excellent video on child abuse. Christie, who had always seemed shy and reserved, made a convicting presentation to our group. After the meeting, a teacher from our local high school who has several family living classes invited Christie to come and make her presentation at the high school. It was exciting to have even a tiny part in encouraging Christie to turn a terrible experience into an opportunity to make a positive difference in our world.

Years ago I read a motivating book by Marion Leach Jacobsen.[1] The thrust of one chapter of her book really had an impact on me. It pointed out that we often sit alone getting more angry, more worried, and more guilty because we are being totally self-centered. We need to get up and get going. The author asserts that you should never complain you are lonely unless during the past week you have:

1. Done at least one kindness for someone who is worse off than you are.
2. Made a telephone call to three individuals to find out how they are getting along — *not* to tell them your troubles.
3. Invited three people to your home, even if just for a cup of coffee or tea.
4. Made plans for at least one activity with someone else.
5. Taken on a responsibility at your church or in your community and done a good job at it.
6. Reached out for new interests, classes, crafts. (Be alive. . . . enthusiastic . . . adventuring!)
7. Read important, stimulating books. (Stay up to date!)
8. Attended organized activities at your church. (They're usually free.)
9. Added a few more items to this list that are guaranteed cures for loneliness.

Practicing Marion Jacobsen's advice can go a long way in lifting our spirits.

KEEP YOUR SENSE OF HUMOR

One of the most important things to remember when you strive to practice hospitality is to keep your sense of humor.

Larry still loves to tell stories about my coffee. Because I don't drink coffee, I really didn't know how to make it. Years ago I made a pot of coffee that our guests had with their dinner, but Larry didn't have until dessert. When he finally tasted it he thought, *My spoon could stand up in this.* He casually asked me how I made the coffee.

"One to one, just like you told me," I replied.

"One what to one what?" he inquired.

"Why, one cup to one cup," I answered him. I had wondered why I had so much trouble fitting all the grounds into the basket.

Larry enjoyed advising me that it was one *tablespoon* of coffee to one *cup* of water, *not* one cup of coffee per cup of water. My coffee did not destroy our relationship with our guests, and we still laugh about that experience. Often the unexpected events that happen when we have guests can turn into great stories later on.

Don't let accidents fluster you. If someone spills an entire glass of sticky juice all over the floor, don't gasp in horror. Just wipe it up. It isn't the end of the world. Remember that people are much more important than sparkling floors or immaculate carpets. How you handle an inconvenience can make a big impression on someone else.

I still remember the evening when something got stuck in my new coffee pot. While we were all bowing quietly in our opening prayer during Bible study, boiling water and coffee grounds flooded all over the counter-top and began dripping onto the floor. We still chuckle when we recall the way we rushed around with towels to stop the water from flowing onto the carpet.

LEARN TO RECEIVE AS WELL AS GIVE

Sometimes it is hard to have a sense of humor about things that go wrong while you are entertaining—or about anything at all. We all go through different "seasons" in our lives, times when we have more or less to give than in other periods. Although practicing hospitality is a directive in Scripture, sometimes we can put out no more than the tiniest efforts.

When nothing at all seems to be available inside, *God wants to encourage us through the hospitality of others.*

Eight years ago when we moved to Indiana, I found myself driving down the road crying. Future friends called and invited us to join them at a hole-in-the-wall diner filled with "local color." That act of kindness did much to encourage me.

A big weakness of mine is putting on a happy face regardless of how I feel inside. It's difficult for me to share my need. There are times when I don't like my husband, my kids, or myself: I just survive. I've had to learn it is all right to stop and let down. If I'm feeling exhausted and drained just when our houseguests are getting their second wind at eleven o'clock at night, I need to excuse myself and go to bed.

When I am emotionally bankrupt and cannot give another ounce, the Lord ministers to me—often through the hospitality of others.

As newlyweds we moved to Illinois and found a friendly church. It was a big help to me to model after those people who so warmly took us in. Receiving from them strengthened me in my ability to give to others.

Remember this important truth: *God knows and cares about each of us individually.* He knows what we have to give and what we need to receive every day. He wants us to relax in the confidence that He is the One who provides for us and for others.

Our ultimate encouragement is Christ Himself. Our sins are forgiven; there are no hoops we have to jump through in order to win a relationship with Him. We are His forever.

One day we are going to attend an eternal party where no one will feel pressured for time, or self-conscious about social flaws, or worried about burning the meal. Someone once said the serious business of heaven is *joy.* Through our hospitality—no, through our *caring,* whatever form it takes—we can give ourselves and others a taste of what is ahead.

As the father of the prodigal must have said to his disgruntled older son, "Come to the party: there's reason to celebrate." And for Christians, that's always true. Our relationship with God and each other has been restored. Hospitality prompted by care and energized by the gospel points to the party that's coming—and that's encouraging.[2]

NOTES
1. Marion Leach Jacobsen, *Crowded Pews and Lonely People* (Wheaton, IL: Tyndale House Publishing, out of print).
2. You may want to read further on this topic in Alexander Strauch's book *Using Your Home For Christ* (Littleton, CO: Lewis & Roth Publishers, 1988).

---❖---

EPILOGUE

Following are thoughts from three women—one married, one single, and one divorced—on aspects of hospitality they have experienced through their relationships with Rachael.

❖

Hospitality has touched me deeply. I am closer to understanding the heart of God as a result of others bringing me into their homes and caring for me.

I do not want to show Rachael as a superwoman who has arrived to some level that mysteriously escapes the rest of us. I do want to honor God who is busy bringing us to our true home. Rachael and others like her, because of Christ's work on the cross, know rest in their hearts and, therefore, are free to offer others drink that satisfies and rest that energizes.

My husband and I have lived with the Crabbs on two different occasions. The first was an experiment in discipleship. We had always wanted to live with an older couple whom we respected. The Crabbs were not only respect worthy (and older) but also willing. My husband and I planned to move in for one month but moved out after four.

The Crabbs were willing to have us again when I became pregnant and was too ill to care for myself. My mom cared for me initially. When it became evident that the situation was going to be long term, Rachael said, "Come move in with us. I'll take care of you." My first reaction was not gratitude; it was panic. That my mom wanted to care for me was understandable and permissible; that my friend wanted to do the same was not. I didn't want Rachael fixing my meals, feeding me, and then cleaning up my vomit. I smile now. . . . She did it many times.

In the past, hospitality had seemed like an event to be endured rather than a lifestyle to be enjoyed. I thought it meant I needed to scrub the house from top to bottom, slave over the perfect menu, and make my husband miserable for not helping me more. The final key was making the guests believe it was no trouble at all. Something is definitely different about how Rachael has had us into her home. Whether she has made a fuss or not, there is a sense that we can find safety, tenderness, and enjoyment.

Instead of making me feel inferior or defeated, watching her has encouraged, challenged, and convicted me. I have been encouraged to listen to my own heart and how I can let goodness be poured out. I do not feel the need to be a "Little Rachael" to be hospitable. I do, however, want to be like Rachael and bend my ear to others' hearts so I can better know how to do them good.

I do not want my hospitality to be out of duty, which can keep me at a distance. I long to be free to invite others into my home so that I can better offer them my heart and the hope that resides within.

Karla

❖

As I begin to write these words about the impact of one specific person's hospitality on my life, my heart wants to express deep gratitude to the numerous other people who have extended hospitality to me. Many others have brought me into their homes, included me in their families, and genuinely cared for me over my life span of a number of years of singleness. All of those encounters have met significant needs as loving demonstrations of the Lord's selfless love for me. The Crabbs' hospitality—which has its origins and energy from deep within the enormously giving heart of Rachael—has also met me at a point of need. But even much more than that, I am marked for life with new clarity of understanding of fundamental truths of God's character, which subsequently prodded me to a deeper desire to radically give myself to others.

I first met Rachael in the spring of 1985, when I traveled to Warsaw for a dear friend's bridal shower. It is still a vivid memory for me. Although Rachael didn't host the event, her enthusiastic participation was a catalyst for making the evening memorable for my friend. It was as though Rachael brought her spirit of hospitality on the road, graphically modeling that the practice of hospitality need not be limited to one's own home. She and I became briefly acquainted that evening, laughing hysterically over the things women laugh about at lingerie showers. Even in the midst of her humor, it was so noticeable to me that every ounce of her energy was focused toward the thrill and joy of the impending marriage of my friend.

Our paths did not cross again until three years later when I returned to Warsaw to visit the same friend—who was now married and the mother of an infant. This time

I came with a fractured arm in a cast and a painfully injured back, physically unable to endure the inviting but uncomfortable sleeping accommodations of my friend's couch. When I arrived at the latest hour of the night—after a long arduous drive from Chicago and a fatiguing week of business travel—Rachael invited me to sleep in her home for the weekend. Though we were still virtually strangers, I was greeted by the fragrance of apple spice, a vase of flowers, a cold pitcher of water by my bed, and a handwritten note of welcome. The next morning I awakened to singing (not hers), homemade blueberry pancakes, and a entertaining breakfast with her family. The mood that pervaded her household was, "Welcome, weary friend. Come and find rest within."

Our next major encounter came in 1988. I was living in Warsaw and, for numerous reasons, was unable to go to my family's home for Christmas. Rachael invited me to join her family. I arrived at her front door in the midst of living an unrelenting frenzied lifestyle. This time I not only presented a weary body but also an exhausted soul. I felt totally bankrupt of any resources with which to give to others. I found the same welcoming, restful mood in her household.

Then the Crabbs invited me to live in their home for a year. This time I was stubbornly committed to not coming empty handed as a burned-out burden! I was determined to be very useful in helping to manage the household affairs while the Crabbs were out of town. After all, I had lived a compentent and responsible life. To enter their home hoping to find an extended period of nourishment and rest seemed to be reverting to a weak and helpless individual. (A perspective I now admit was immature.)

But with arms outstretched, Rachael's invitation to me—as it has been to countless others—was simply,

"Come and *relax!* Allow us to come alongside you and share your burden for a while. Taste of the lifegiving *rest* that God desires for you and how He longs to *enjoy* a relationship with you that is based on His character, not on your usefulness." That invitation has had an especially powerful impact on my heart as a woman who often finds herself heavily weighted down (sometimes unnecessarily so) by the burdensome task of living life alone.

It took time, loving confrontations, and tender experiences for my stubborn, independent, arrogant heart to be shattered, to realize that God desires for me a far richer and more *restful* relationship with Him than I had ever understood, that He longed to be my advocate in ways I had not yet grasped.

What I learned from Rachael is that hospitality has less to do with the physical provisions and more to do with the way a person feels in your presence—that they can rest and experience a brief oasis. When a person is encouraged, refreshed, and revitalized, becoming confident of the future rest that awaits them in eternity because of the sacrifice of Christ, then they have been wooed closer to the character of God by the practice of hospitality.

The nature of the Crabbs' hospitality toward me has been both loving and confronting, always beckoning me to look upward and outward to the hope and the rest that Jesus offers. Hospitality that has this focus at its core can be offered by all or us.

Judy

❖

When the book *Encouragement: The Key to Caring* by Larry Crabb was published, I read it with fervor. I felt the local church could encourage and care in more practical ways than what I had experienced. At that time, I lived in the same town as the Crabbs but didn't know them nor thought I ever would.

A few years later, however, my husband and I started attending the same church as the Crabbs. We were having marital problems, and I remember thinking as I met Larry, "I wonder if we'll ever get to know this man and if he'll have an influence on our lives and marriage."

About a year later, I was thrilled when Rachael asked me if I would consider involvement in the women's ministry and be the hospitality coordinator at our church. That was the beginning of getting to know Rachael as we worked together and had some creative and fun ministry times. As the stress from my marital problems intensified, I felt I needed to resign from my position, and that's when Rachael learned of the severity of the situation. Larry was still only a "smile and greeting" acquaintance, but he extended a warm, genuine invitation to me to stay with them, as if we had been friends for some time.

Hospitality doesn't have to be gourmet meals and fine china. It doesn't have to be playing games every second to keep the company entertained. I have seen it lived out in accepting you for who you are, where you are, and treating you like you're a person of value. This can be done in the smallest ways.

One day, Rachael and I were cooking in her kitchen, and I asked where a spatula was. "Oh, I don't have one," she replied. The next day she purchased a spatula . . . for me. A little gesture, but one that touched me deeply.

Rachael's creative, teaching background is reflected in her house around holidays. Once as we sat looking over her Valentine decorations, I made a casual comment on a heart that was to be hung in the window. As she was deciding where to place everything she said, "Here, this one's for your room since you said you liked it." The fact that she took notice of my casual comment and gave it some priority as well as placing it in "my room" — not the *guest* room — made me feel warm and loved.

A few little acts of kindness, but only I and my heavenly Father know of the big part they had in beginning my healing process. He is the Potter and I am the clay that can be reshaped and restored. I really feel that heartfelt hospitality can be an important factor in the restoration of shattered pottery.

Cheryl